To clear the confusion that exists in the minds of many Christians concerning the value of religious belief in the conduct of their lives, Dr. Smart has written this book which tells laymen in simple and understandable language just what the Scriptures should lead them to believe. The author reasons that although good conduct springs from sound religious belief, this in itself does not constitute real religion. Since behavior results from ideas, sound convictions are the father of well-organized action. For that reason man's understanding of what the Bible says about him is essential.

Dr. Smart takes the position that doctrine, explained in plain language, affords the average layman the answers to most of the questions that have been puzzling him. In these answers lie the solutions to problems common to our daily life, our faith, and our relationships to family, friends, and life as a whole.

What A Man Can Believe

WHAT A MAN CAN BELIEVE

JAMES D. SMART: *Minister of St. Paul's
Presbyterian Church, Peterborough, Ontario*

Philadelphia: THE WESTMINSTER PRESS

Preface

THROUGHOUT THE CHURCH, men are beginning
to recognize that something is wrong, seriously wrong,
in regard to doctrine. A critical hour has come upon us
unawares, like a thief in the night, and has caught us
unprepared. Instead of a clear and powerful word
sounding forth from the Church into the confusion of
our times, there is found almost as much confusion in
the word of the Church as in the world. Why is this so?
I am convinced that it is because in our modern Church
there has taken place over a long period of years a
mingling of faiths which in essence are contradictory.
In the theological realm this mingling can be traced
most plainly in the developments from the time of
Schleiermacher on. Views of God and man, and of the
world, which originated not in the Hebrew tradition
but in the Greek, not in the Christian revelation but in
the non-Christian philosophies, became incorporated
into the Church's theology. Then by successfully repre-
senting themselves as the original Christian ideas, they
have managed to pass into the mind of the Church.

An example will make plain what is meant.

The view of man as a being of divine capacities, with a lower nature which must be kept under, but with a higher nature which ever reaches out for truth, beauty, goodness, and God, prevails very widely in our time. It is taken for granted that this is what a Christian must believe concerning man. We are sinful, erring creatures, yet nevertheless, as Bernard Iddings Bell puts it in his *O Men of God,* " competent to tower above circumstances, capable of reaching out and up " until we catch a glimpse of God. " There must be proclamation with glad voice from the pulpit, in the shop and on the street corner, of the good news of man's true dignity." This is the view of man which strikes a responsive chord in our modern age.

But it must be recognized that this is not the Biblical view of man, which despairs utterly of the capacities and possibilities of man as he is by nature. To be sure, the Biblical view does not deny that by nature man has a wisdom and a spirituality, but it does assert that something has happened to human nature which, in spite of all that may be said in praise of it, makes it incapable of its true life until in Christ it is made a new creation. It is still worth our while to ask what measure of truth may lie behind the assertion found in Gen., ch. 3, that at the center of man's life one finds not a seeking and reaching out of the soul toward God (that is how man

likes to think of himself, idealistically and sentimen-
tally), but a determined evasion by man of *God's search*
for him. The New Testament assumes throughout that
man is a creature alienated and estranged from God.
It is significant that this Biblical teaching concerning
man has often of late been branded as primitive and
crude, unacceptable to our enlightened modern mind.
And yet, is this not merely an attempt to excuse the repudiation of original Christian convictions and the substitution for them of a more congenial view? There
remains, however, in the Church, a dim remembrance
of what the Scriptures say concerning man.

The sum effect, however, of contradictory views of
man existing side by side, undistinguished, and often
proclaimed in a mingled form from the same pulpit, is
a paralyzing confusion in the mind and life of the
Church. The task of theology in our day is to do something about this confusion, to set itself as a guard and
watchman over the Church's life, and to rid it of the
other faiths which, disguised as Christian, have slipped
in unnoticed. Theology can perform that task only as it
recalls the Church to the message of the Scriptures.
Only where that message sounds in its purity as a living
and redeeming word can there be a perception of the
line between light and darkness, between truth and
falsehood.

This book is an attempt to do something about that

confusion of faiths, but at a lower level than that of the theologian, namely, at the level of the man in the pew. The mingling of contradictory faiths is not by any means the exclusive concern of the academic theologian. It has its fruits in the lives of countless Christian people. Its ultimate effects are to be seen in the social, economic, and political events of our time. The confusion in the Church's faith has a closer connection than we realize with the seeming lack in our world of any power adequate to restrain the forces of evil. The average Christian is aware of the powerlessness of the Church and of Christianity. Yet he is not aware that such powerlessness is due to the fact that *in him* another faith has imperceptibly substituted itself for the Christian faith. What passes for faith in God, in Christ, in the Holy Spirit, in the Church, is something that on the surface looks like Christian faith, but has nothing of its true nature.

My purpose is therefore to show what faith means in the terms of the Scriptures, that thereby the common man may see more clearly the line between a true and a false faith, and be recalled out of his superficial religiousness or irreligiousness into a living and fruitful faith. The aim is not to secure a new orthodoxy of ideas — that would be as barren as our recent heterodoxy and much less charitable — but simply to let the message of the Scriptures be heard, that it may sound in

our ears as a word both of judgment and of promise.
The underlying conviction is that if we would let God's
truth loose among us, unchained and undistorted, we
should soon see the changes coming about, both in the
Church and in the world, which we so much desire.

J. D. S.

PETERBOROUGH, ONTARIO
OCTOBER, 1943

Contents

PREFACE   3

1. Does It Matter What We Believe?   13
2. How Can We Believe?   35
3. The Word of God   61
4. God the Father Almighty   87
5. Jesus Christ, His Son   109
6. Christ Crucified   127
7. The Holy Spirit   147
8. The Church of Christ   167
9. The Forgiveness of Sins   193
10. The Life Everlasting   225

CONCLUSION   251

Chapter 1

Does It Matter What We Believe?

It has been an accepted principle in the Church for some time that the surest method of putting most Christians to sleep is to begin talking to them about beliefs, doctrines, creeds, or theology. It may seem perilous, therefore, in a book that is meant for the common man — that is, the man who is unlearned in theology — to begin with a discussion of those reputedly sleep-compelling words. But this idea that the rank and file of Christians are not interested in deeper questions of doctrine is the result of a superficial estimate of man. Of course, a man goes to sleep if doctrines are discussed in language that is completely beyond his range, just as a sportsman who is thoroughly interested in dogs would go to sleep if a biologist tried to talk to him about dogs in scientific terminology. But that does not mean that interest in the subject is lacking. Let the questions of Christian doctrine be stated in plain language, and the layman recognizes at once that they are *his* questions, the problems of life and faith with which he has to grapple day after day.

13

Creeds and Theology

The words " creed " and " theology " have been badly knocked about of late, until in our day they are almost ashamed to show their heads in a public place. They find it safer to hide away in the restful seclusion of a theological classroom. Strangely, they have received their hardest knocks in Christian Churches at the hands of professedly broad-minded preachers and teachers. The word " creed " has been most bitterly attacked, with the result that for multitudes who have never even read a creed the word suggests a narrow and confining bigotry. But these men who declaim against creeds are doing so on the basis of a creed of their own, although the statement of their own creed may still be in a vague and indefinite stage. The most dogmatic people one meets are always those who condemn all dogma, just as in the name of tolerance men will be fiercely intolerant of any other viewpoint than their own self-styled tolerant one. A creed is simply a statement of what a man, or a Church of men, believes, and a man without a creed would be a man who believes nothing. Such a being, it is safe to state, has never yet appeared in human flesh. Honesty demands, therefore, that instead of reviling all creeds under a pretense of broad-mindedness, men should be content to state wherein their own creed differs from that of another man or that of the Church.

The word " theology " has been made to suggest something not so much harsh or narrow as remote from practical life. When the minister leaves his hearers behind him and soars through tracts unknown, they assume charitably but mistakenly that he is spreading his wings in distant " theological " regions, whither it is neither possible nor very profitable for mere laymen to venture. It is unfortunate that laymen should have this impression that theology is religion in a form that is far above their heads and far beyond their powers of comprehension. Theology, when it knows its task, is related at every point to practical life. It is not concerned with abstruse philosophical speculations, but with the thorny questions with which the man in the pew has to deal as soon as he begins to take seriously his relationship to God, to himself, and to his fellow men. For a man to say that he is not interested in theology is an admission that he is not interested in truth, and that he is not aware how much his life is determined by those convictions that he holds as true.

Occasionally, we hear it announced that, in spite of all appearances of irreligiousness in our age, religion remains the first interest of man. Midnight conversations of men in college have a way of gravitating toward religious questions. Wherever a group of people are engaged in conversation for any length of time, religion is likely to come up in some way for discussion. It could not be otherwise, for, after all, the chief thing a man does is to live. His own inner life, his relationship to those about him, and his relationship to life as a whole are naturally his primary interests, taking precedence over all others. And it is to these three questions that Christianity professes to have the answers. Formal theology is the attempt to talk of these questions and answers in scientific, full-dress language. But when the ordinary man talks of these same questions in plain-clothes language, he also is engaging in theology.

It seems a little absurd that it should be necessary to discuss whether or not beliefs matter. In wide areas of the world today the conviction holds sway that nothing matters quite so much as what men believe. Communists have learned the importance of doctrine for practical life, and, in order to safeguard certain forms of life that they have created, they are enforcing a rigid orthodoxy in ideas. Similarly in Germany, Italy, and Japan, " dangerous thoughts " are recognized as subversive to the state and are strictly excluded from the country if possible. This is an ignorant method of dealing with ideas, not likely to prove effective over a long period, but behind it is at least the knowledge that ideas are of more practical consequence than anything else, that ideas determine events.

70001

Yet within the Christian Church there prevails a rank carelessness about ideas and beliefs. The problems of *doctrinal* training are not given very serious consideration by the Church. The Church's emphasis is upon activity and conduct rather than upon ideas. Parents do not concern themselves that the beliefs forming in their children's lives may be truly Christian. They train their children in Christian conduct, and leave this more difficult and elusive matter of beliefs to the mercies of a few fleeting minutes in a Sunday School. And then they exclaim against those children in indignation and amazement when later they take to themselves other than Christian beliefs, which produce something other than the Christian life. There are indications at a dozen points in the Church's life that most Christians are unaware of the importance of ideas and beliefs. Consequently they fail to give to this aspect of their faith the attention and careful consideration that it deserves.

A Wrong Emphasis Upon Beliefs

It has been a misfortune of the first order that the adherents of a superpious, holier-than-thou type of Christianity have become known as those who are most interested in beliefs and doctrines. They link together a very narrow conception of the Christian life with an intense strictness about right beliefs. They have told the world so often that they are the sole defenders of the " full Gospel faith " that the world is indisposed to hear them for their much speaking. The result has been that, crediting these folk with the orthodoxy which they claim, most men form a low estimate of the " full Gospel faith " from the kind of defense that is made for it. These advocates of strong doctrine are noted for their ability to produce arguments, with which they prove conclusively to themselves the reasonableness of their religious views, but convince no one who does not already hold their point of view.

The acceptance of correct beliefs is, in this familiar type of zealous religiousness, an indispensable condition of salvation. Usually a list is drawn up of all that it is necessary for a Christian man to believe — a quite long list — and with different representatives of this general point of view the details of the list may show extensive variations. Some are certain that all who do not believe in baptism by immersion are eternally damned. Others omit this, but insist upon a like importance for some particular interpretation of the Second Coming of Christ. All assert a doctrine of the literal inerrancy of the Scriptures, and often make this the touchstone by which they discriminate between believers and nonbelievers. The salvation of man is made directly dependent upon his holding of a code of right doctrines. When we ask how one comes to an acceptance of such doctrines, we are told that anyone who has been soundly converted should have no difficulty with their acceptance. The fact that we do not understand any doctrine is not regarded as just cause for withholding assent. Any serious questioning of the doctrines in their commonly held meanings is taken at once as the mark of an unregenerate soul. Discussion between those who hold this point of view and other Christians is fundamentally impossible; their attitude excludes it. Either a man is a believer (in their sense of the word) or he is an unbeliever. And if he is an unbeliever, the only sensible thing to do is to attempt to convert him, or, failing that, to condemn him.

Most Christians have come in contact with religion of this kind, and have reacted against it, usually with no clear idea of what it is that offends them. They are convinced that it is not necessary to adopt such an attitude in order to be a Christian, but they might have difficulty in saying what is unchristian in it. They know only that they do not like it, and, rejecting it with somewhat violent emotion, they fall into a very unsympathetic attitude toward all attempts to lay emphasis upon beliefs. This is the great misfortune — that concern about beliefs has become identified so closely with an untenable religious viewpoint that widespread repudiation of that viewpoint throughout the Church has brought with it a disinclination on the part of Christian people to give any attention to the subject of Christian beliefs.

This exalting of doctrinal formulas into a code of infallible truths must be dealt with as it deserves. We repudiate it, not because we want freedom to believe as we please and are unwilling to acknowledge any authority in regard to truth beyond that of our own reason, but because we see in it a usurping of the authority that belongs only to God in his Word. Creeds, which were meant to be humble guides directing men to the truth of God, cannot be allowed to become harsh despots coercing men into right beliefs under threat of eternal punishment. The God who speaks to us in the Scriptures does not damn us for our doubts or insist at any point in his revelation of himself that our welfare in time and eternity is dependent upon an immediate assent to a detailed list of doctrines. He knows too well that for human life there can never be any completeness in the knowledge of the truth. Even a Paul can see only dim images as in a darkened mirror. Therefore, when mere men presume to speak of Christian truths with an air of complete self-confidence and pronounce upon them with finality, we have good reason to draw back from them and to view their handling of the Christian faith with distrust.

If it were God's will that the question of truth should be set at rest in this simple manner, it is strange that none of his prophets, or wise men, or apostles, or even Jesus, should have provided men with an appropriate code of beliefs. How much more satisfactory that would have been than what Jesus did, merely promising to his disciples the Spirit, who would lead them into all truth! An infallible code, with Jesus' imprimatur upon it, would have saved the Church centuries of muddling about between truth and error, and would have made unnecessary all the labor which has been expended in efforts to make clear the nature of Christian truth. One would expect that Paul, who was so much concerned about sound doctrine, would have hit upon this simple expedient by which sound doctrine could so easily have been ensured. In the New Testament we can detect the first outlines of a Christian creed in which the Church sought to express its faith, but we can find no suggestion of a detailed and infallibly authoritative statement of faith. Surely this ought to convince us that dealing with the question of beliefs in a dictatorial manner and pressing certain views upon men as the only legitimate Christian formulations are in themselves non-Christian practices.

It would be wrong to give the impression that we have nothing to learn from these people who give such an undue place to beliefs. As a rule they put all others in the Church to shame by the energy and earnestness of their religion. However unsatisfactory their attitude regarding beliefs may be, at least they do believe something with definiteness. The Christian faith as they present it has a distinct shape and form. They know where they stand as Christians, and they let others know where they stand. In their naïve fashion, at least they do listen to hear the message of the Scriptures, and from this issues a certain forcefulness in their Christian living and their Christian witness. The more moderate and reasonable type of Christianity prevalent in the Churches seems a poor, weak, dumb thing in comparison. One can understand why earnest souls, hungering for a living, wholehearted, and clear-cut Christian faith, have sometimes turned in this other direction, even though it meant putting severe blinders upon their minds. Sometimes the integrity of the mind seems a small price to pay for a living faith. But the mind ultimately revenges itself by entangling faith in intellectual absurdities and so bringing disrepute and ostracism upon it. That, however, does not prevent us from making the admission that the source of much of our weakness and ineffectiveness in the Church is our uncertainty about where we stand and our confusion about what we believe.

The Place of Beliefs in the Shaping of Life

It is almost inconceivable that it should be so, but it is true that the commonest attitude in the Church today is that beliefs do not matter much — that is, they are of no very great *practical* importance. One of the watchwords of our day is that it is not what a man *believes* but what he *is* that counts in life. The emphasis is laid upon the word " life," to the disparagement of all that can be placed under the category of theory. Character is the great interest, and the building of character the primary function of the Church. " Tell us what to be and how to be it rather than what to believe," say men. But a man does not need to be a Christian in order to perceive the superficiality of that approach to life. As soon as he begins to probe into the sources of character and conduct, he becomes aware how much life is shaped and influenced by the convictions of the mind, whether they be intelligent convictions or mere prejudices and fancies. The writer of The Proverbs speaks truth when he says that " As a man thinketh in his heart, so is he." It is impossible to distinguish between what a man thinks and believes and what he is. The two are inseparable parts of a single whole. Our thoughts and ideas and beliefs determine the nature of our characters and give the pattern to our conduct.

The importance of beliefs for practical life can be shown with reasonable clearness in a sphere where most persons have experience, in regard to love and marriage. A high-pitched, romantic idea of love has received wide currency in our day. It is pressed upon youth from every side, and is such in its nature that it does not require much pressing for youth to accept it unreservedly.

The idea, briefly, is that to find one's destined partner in life is to find the key to happiness. Human love gives a solution to life's problems, sets a man free to live his true life, and in general brings human nature to its consummation. In short, romantic love becomes a kind of religion, for that which is expected of it is that which, our religion claims, can be found only in God. A result is sought from the fellowship of two human personalities that can be produced only by the fellowship of man with his God. Because what is experienced in the human relationship suggests what may be possible in the higher relationship, man is led on to seek in the human that which by its nature it is not able to give.

But as long as a man or woman retains in mind this romantic, idealistic expectation, severe injustice must be done to the human relationship. Disillusionment concerning the chosen partner in love may bring bitterness and despair. There are people who are merely tolerating each other in marriage because with the fading of the first glow of their love there entered in the fatal suspicion that they were not " destined partners." This has been the underlying cause of many divorces. A strain is put upon human love and human nature which they are not able to endure, and a result is anticipated from marriage which of itself it cannot produce. Romantic love is an attitude toward one of life's most sacred relationships that makes disillusionment with it inevitable.

By contrast, the Christian point of view might be termed a sane realism. Disillusionment of a serious nature is impossible, for, in spite of all the ecstasies of love, the truth is not forgotten that human nature is sinful. Marriage is a union of two sinful persons, which does not automatically cancel the power of sin to create ill consequences in life. Marriage is entered upon with a full realization that the natural love of man and woman is not sufficient to meet life's situations. Another love, the love of God, which conquers human egotism and gives to mortals the spirit that forgives even seventy times seven, is alone sufficient. And this love can be man's possession, not as his own achievement, but only as his response to a love which meets him in Jesus Christ, and in him alone. " We love . . . because he first loved us." It can be seen, then, that in this sphere the ideas and beliefs that dominate the mind are of primary importance in determining the conduct of life, and carelessness about them is a carelessness about life itself.

Taking Our Beliefs for Granted

We have now dealt with two common attitudes toward our subject which stand in contrast to each other.

There remains a third, perhaps the commonest of all, and certainly the most dangerous of all, because it seems to follow a sensible middle course, avoiding the extremes. It consists in taking for granted that such beliefs as are held by most Christians are quite adequate, and that there is no great need to bother oneself overmuch about them. Many a Christian, without giving much thought to the matter, assumes the essential integrity of his own religious views. Even Christian ministers not infrequently are guilty of attributing a certain finality to the religious point of view which has by various influences in the course of the years become theirs. They show little or no interest in reaching out beyond to a wider and fuller truth. The result always is a closed mind and a stagnant faith. The Holy Spirit, who is to lead us into all truth, is not likely to make much headway with men who think they have already arrived.

It is easy for any one of us to assume a position such as this: " I believe all that any Christian need believe and I am an earnest God-fearing man; what more can be expected? " But that evades the critical question, Have we examined our beliefs and principles so that we know clearly what they are, and have we any reason for confidence that they are Christian? We are all of us children of our age, and subject in the formation of our minds to the streams of influences that predominate in our age. Tendencies of various kinds carry us with them, often without any conscious choice on our part. In all these things, and from sources in our own natures, truth and falsehood build themselves into our thought world and into our character.

However earnest we are, we are certain to go aside from the truth. It is in the very nature of all things human that we can never have truth without an admixture of falsehood. Therefore, a smug attitude of uncritical contentment is in reality disloyalty to the truth. It is an evasion by the Christian of his duty of watching over the soul's fortress that the forces of error may not slip in unawares. Pious acceptance of Christian doctrines followed by unconcern is more dangerous to the Church than definite antagonism and opposition to its doctrines. It is that kind of piety which, as Samuel Butler says, is shocked to hear the Christian faith doubted, and equally surprised to see it practiced. There are many Christians who would repel with indignation the charge of indifference about beliefs. They are greatly concerned that right beliefs should be held and they show their concern by being horrified whenever they hear of people who hold wrong beliefs. They value sound doctrine very highly and regard themselves as models of it. But they have not interested themselves enough even to have seen with any clearness the nature of the problems that are involved.

The Incoherence of Present-Day Christianity

The incoherence of Christian people is one of the most striking features of present-day Christianity. Faith seems to lack the power of utterance, not only in addressing men, but also in speaking to God in prayer. This is sometimes excused by saying that the things of faith lie too deep and are too sacred for utterance, that to attempt to put such things in words would debase them. It is true that religious speech is always beset by the peril of becoming mere pious babbling. Yet, perilous as it is, it must be dared. The silent witness of what a man is is not enough. Faith must speak out sincerely and plainly if it is not to be as a light hidden under a bushel measure. It must be recognized that lack of this power to speak out is not just a failing of a few individual Christians, but is characteristic of a type of religion which prevails widely in our generation.

It will, perhaps, make clear what is meant if we consider the predicament of the average Christian, a man who has been reared in a Christian home, has attended Sunday School and Church, and has come to be recognized as a fine example of Christian character. Unexpectedly and all unforewarned, he has been cornered by a person seeking in earnest the meaning of Christian faith. To the question, " How can I find God? " what

answer shall he give? Confronted by the naked need
of a human soul, what more will be forthcoming than
the sympathy of a genuine kindliness and a desire to
help? Many in that situation would find themselves embarrassed, and their only resource would be to send the
person to a minister. They can talk about religion in a
casual, objective fashion, but when it becomes a living
thing in which a human soul is at stake, it is as though
they were tongue-tied.

The neglect in recent years of the " knowledge " side
of religion is largely responsible for this incoherence.
Many factors enter in: the transference of religious education from the home to the Sunday School, the decline
of Bible-reading, the emphasis upon the practical and
the inspirational to the neglect of the doctrinal in religion. The sum effect has been to rob us of the ability
to speak simply and sincerely in witness to our faith.

There is an old saying that a man with virtue but without knowledge is like a soldier with a shield but without
a sword: He has the means wherewith to protect himself but none with which to help his fellow. That describes accurately the situation of many Christian people. They have virtues which preserve their own lives
from temptation and evil, virtues of which not a few
have come down as a heritage from a past generation,
but they have not the knowledge that would enable them
to guide others to the sources of virtue. They are liv-

ing upon the spiritual inheritance of the past, an inheritance of character and standards which have been taken
over without any definite understanding of their source
and basis. But these qualities of character and standards
of life, as they are passed on from generation to generation, gradually lose their power and their meaning.
They become sacred but essentially incomprehensible
relics of a bygone age, and are unable to shape the life
of a new generation.

The conception of Christianity that predominates at
present in many minds is that it is chiefly concerned with
being good and doing good. The ethical interest out-
weighs, if it does not at times exclude, all others. Of
course, the standard of what is meant by " good " varies
with each individual. It may mean not drinking too
much, being reasonably decent to his wife and children,
and doing enough kind acts to assure him of the essential charitableness of his own soul; or it may mean a
high standard of purity and integrity and unselfish living. Again it may cause a man to interest himself in social questions, that he may understand how to be good,
not just individually, but socially. Conduct in this instance is interpreted in its wider aspects. But in every
case the moral interest is central and the tendency is to
make of Christianity a moralism instead of a faith. The
concern of parents is that their children may be good
rather than that they should come to a knowledge of
the truth which makes one free. Truth is definitely rele-

gated to second place, or even farther off than that. It is thought to be sufficient — in fact all that can be desired — if by some means the end can be secured that children, young people, and grown people shall be good.

The situation in the Christian home is to be understood in this light. Intelligent, believing parents often leave completely untouched the task which at baptism they promised to fulfill — to instruct their children in the truths and duties of the Christian faith. In early years the children have Bible stories read to them and they are taught one or two simple prayers. As their minds become more capable of understanding and life becomes more complex and difficult, the parents fail to continue with instruction appropriate to the need. Few parents seem to feel any responsibility whatever in this regard, or, if they do, they shrink from the task. If they think that the Sunday School relieves them of the responsibility, they are sadly mistaken. It is incapable of providing adequate instruction.

There is no substitute for the parent in the work of religious education. Nevertheless, the idea that questions of truth are not of first importance apparently holds sway with most Christian parents. Character and conduct receive all the attention and the deeper serious questionings of the mind in childhood and youth are passed by as though they did not exist. The inevitable result is that a generation is being turned loose into life with no firm convictions and with no knowledge of the why and

wherefore of its faith. It is not to be wondered at that
many have cut themselves adrift from the traditions in
which they were trained. Morality, when its foundations in Christian knowledge are gone, has not much
to hold it up. Even the broadest socialized morality
cannot stand by itself. When Christianity degenerates
into a moralism, it is not long before life grows fretful
in that hollow shell of morality and tries in impatience
to throw it off. There is ultimately nothing that can
conquer, direct, and liberate life except truth. And the
question of truth is the question of beliefs.

All life proceeds from beliefs of some kind. We may
not always be conscious what they are, but they are there
as the substratum of all our living. The question is not,
Shall we have beliefs? but, What beliefs have we? Behind a man's actions there is always to be found a certain general attitude toward life, certain basic convictions. For instance, if he does not believe that God is
good, then he believes that he is bad, or indifferent, or
in God's place he sets a blind Fate. And whatever a man
believes about God affects his whole outlook upon life.
Similarly, in regard to his fellow men, he has to believe something, for life forces him into human relationships. What he believes will determine the nature
of his existence as a social being. The problem of beliefs cannot be evaded, for it is the problem of existence.

Chapter 2

How Can We Believe?

THAT WE PROPOSE to investigate this subject of our Christian beliefs may appear to some a presumptuous and superfluous undertaking. Have not such matters as these been settled by the giants of our faith in the days of long ago? What can the pygmies of modern times hope to add to the wisdom stored up for us by the Fathers of the Church. We have the historic creeds of the Church and our own revered Confession of Faith. Do they not decide once and for all the essentials of our faith so that there can be neither an adding to it nor a taking away from it?

The Ever Unfinished Task

We speak of *questions* of belief, but, if the above be sound, there can be no very great concern about the questions, for the answers are already there, and have been there a long time, to be read plainly by all who are willing to read. This attitude may seem to exhibit a commendable reverence for the Church's past and loyalty to its traditions. In reality it is a stupid, unintelligent formalism, only a short step removed from the

35

establishing of a historic confession in a position of absolute dictatorship within the Church. Its general effect is to submerge freedom of inquiry in the Church to a level about equal to that enjoyed by Roman Catholics. In fact, the parallels between Roman Catholicism and the types of Protestantism in which the attempt is made to establish the absolute authority of the letter of a creed or the letter of the Scriptures are most striking. They all appeal to that in man which longs to be completely free of spiritual questionings. It *is* painful to be undecided, until one sees that in some things one must be undecided if one is to be honest. The human mind and spirit do not exert themselves except under compulsion. The possibility of a quick and ready-made solution to the problem of what to believe appeals to a well-known weakness in our natures. It appeals to our weakness, and not to our strength.

The existence of a Confession of Faith which our Church owns as its standard, and which we personally recognize as our standard, does not settle with finality the question of what we are to believe today. To raise it to a place where it dictates to us what our beliefs *must* be, without any opportunity for discussion or appeal, is a misuse, or, to use a stronger and more fitting word, a *perverted* use, of the creed. Such perversions have been partially responsible for the ill repute into which creeds and confessions have come.

The men who at certain critical points in the history of the Church formulated the Church's faith into creeds had no intention of relieving us of the responsibility of facing, in our own day and age, the great questions that have to do with the meaning of the Christian faith. They were discharging their own responsibility of stating as sincerely and completely as was possible what they, in their day and situation, had to believe as Christian men. They were witnessing as men to the truth of God which had come to them, and the purpose of their witness was primarily to give men guidance into that truth, not to compel men to believe. It is not to be denied that often compulsion was attempted. The pointing finger when not obeyed had a tendency to contract, under the force of impatience, into a threatening fist. The agelong weakness of all enthusiasts for the truth is that they cannot wait, as Jesus was ready to wait, for the slow process of germination, growth, and fruition of the truth in the souls of men. But that leaves untouched the assertion that the intention of the creeds was guidance, and not compulsion.

It is truly a serious matter that we are neglecting the guidance of the creeds today. A scientist or mathematician or historian who refused to be instructed by those who had gone before him, and who failed to examine the answers they gave to his questions, would be remiss in his duty and would court failure. If we are in earnest about seeking and finding Christian truth, we shall not despise any guidance that can come to us from the past. We shall not share the common optimism about modern enlightenment, which supposes man to have reached a stage of knowledge in which he has little or nothing of importance to learn from men of older days. Rather, we are inclined to say that man today has lost a knowledge that men of an older day possessed. There is need for us to turn to the past, not slavishly, but with willingness to be taught. It is quite possible that if we were to go back to the guideposts that are provided by the creeds and seek our way in the direction in which they point us, we modern men might find a surer road through the maze of our perplexities and obstacles.

The creeds remind us that we are not the first who have asked the great, deep questions of faith. There is a reassurance in that. These are the questions with which Christians have been concerned from the very beginning, and upon which the Church has had to pronounce, not once, but many times. Therefore we approach the creeds reverently and humbly. But we accept no historic creed as an absolute and final arbiter of beliefs. There is no ready-made solution to *our* question of beliefs. Nothing can lift from us the responsibility of undertaking our own pilgrimage in search of the truth, to determine in our life situation of today what *we* believe. We dare not say, " Our father's beliefs are good enough for us," although there is a sense in which it may be true. If our fathers had strong and clear-cut Christian beliefs, it was to a large extent because they were not satisfied to take truth secondhand but sought it earnestly and found it for themselves. Secondhand beliefs are never more than half beliefs. They might even be termed make-beliefs with considerable justification. We do not ask freedom to believe as we like, but freedom to seek the truth in the only way in which it is ever found. We ask to see the truth for ourselves before we call it true. We assert our right to acknowledge no absolute authority except that of God himself in his truth.

It is not a new truth we seek, but rather the rediscovery of an old truth. There are some who with Promethean spirit feel that our only hope is to " interrogate the Universe afresh." Others are confident that the only truths we can trust are those that are being revealed by the modern scientific investigation of human life. But, strangely, these fresh interrogations of the universe and modern investigations of life seem to result in religious viewpoints that are in their essential characteristics as old as the hills. We suspect, with reason, that the basic presuppositions were not deduced, but were assumed. And when the lack of continuity with New Testament Christianity becomes an embarrassment, we begin to suspect that it may be more fruitful and more in order to seek an old truth called " Christian " than a new truth which it is difficult to label. And because it is an old truth we seek, we are ready to listen to those who in the past have been in earnest about it, and who profess to have found it and to have lived by it.

Here, then, is where we stand. We are certain that right beliefs are essential to the Christian life. We accept the creeds of the past, not as final statements of what Christians must always believe, but as guideposts for succeeding generations, to point them in the direction in which truth is to be found. We assert the right and the duty of every Christian to inquire for himself into this question of truth, affirming that the answers of men in other days, however great the measure of truth in them, are not adequate to be our answers today; that we in the twentieth century must state what we, as a Church built upon the prophets and apostles and with Jesus Christ as its chief cornerstone, believe to be the truth of the Christian Gospel. Right in the midst of the peculiar problems of our day, and with direct bearing upon them, the old truths must be brought out into the open and become new.

The Superficiality of Current Skepticism

If the extreme orthodox element within the Church would deny our right to treat the subject of beliefs as an open question, from without the Church another group arises which would deny us even the right *to believe*. Accordingly, if we persist, and believe anything at all, there is pronounced upon us a kind of intellectual excommunication. The prevailing intellectual winds of our day are steadily against all definite Christian beliefs. Few within the Church are aware what a force skepticism and agnosticism have in our secular education. There would be no objection were it merely the natural skepticism and agnosticism of the scholar who questions all things and by questioning them develops the power of discrimination. But it is not that. It is, generally speaking, a certain acquired attitude of dogmatic skepticism which takes as the first article of its creed that Christian beliefs are no longer tenable for an intelligent man. A new standard of intellectual respectability has been established which a student must defy if he is to take a positive stand in regard to any Christian belief. There has come into existence an orthodoxy of agnosticism which is as narrow and dogmatic as any Church orthodoxy. Moreover, it has the same effect of discouraging the search for truth. Church orthodoxy says, " There is no need to investigate, for all Christian truth has been found." Agnostic orthodoxy says, " There is no need to investigate, for there is no Christian truth to find."

Consequently, many people find themselves in the

situation of wishing they could believe, but feeling sad and hopeless, because they are certain that for them Christian beliefs have become an impossibility. Joseph Wood Krutch, in *The Modern Temper* (1930), asserts this to be characteristic of the intellectual life of our day. He speaks of a "longing of soul for its old spiritual constructions," which, however, is doomed never to be satisfied. He sees his age as one that is unable to achieve either religious belief on the one hand or exultant atheism on the other.

But why should any man take a fatalistic attitude of this kind in regard to religious belief? Is it really good logic, on the basis of the fact that he does not believe, to assert that he can never believe? This tragic attitude, not indeed in Krutch, but as we find it reproducing itself in countless young people, becomes a kind of romantic pose. It is very romantic to feel oneself hopelessly adrift, with all the old ties irreparably cut — sad, but at the same time pleasant and thrilling. If the spiritual longing has any real earnestness in it, it should cause a man, not to dismiss Christianity with a superficial consideration, but to delve into it, seeking what meaning it may have for him. It is significant that today, because of the prevalent agnosticism, we have to plead that Christianity may at least be accorded a hearing as a subject worthy of the consideration of thinking men.

The prophets of this new agnostic orthodoxy are

legion, and their influence is as pervasive and compelling as a new style in women's hats. It may be instructive to examine a few of the most eminent of its prophets, who set the style in irreligion, and to ask upon what basis they dismiss Christianity as an outworn religion.

First let us hear Bertrand Russell (*Living Philosophies,* pp. 9 ff.): "I continued to believe devoutly in the Unitarian faith until the age of fourteen, at which period I became exceedingly religious and consequently anxious to know whether there was any good ground for supposing religion to be true. For the next four years a great part of my time was spent in secret meditation upon this subject; *I could not speak to anybody about it* [our italics] for fear of giving pain. I suffered acutely, both from the gradual loss of faith and from the necessity of silence." He cast off belief in free will, then in immortality. "I continued to believe in God until the age of eighteen, since the First Cause argument appeared to me irrefutable. At eighteen, however, the reading of Mill's autobiography showed me the fallacy in this argument. I therefore definitely abandoned all the dogmas of Christianity, and to my surprise I found myself much happier than while I had been struggling to retain some sort of theological belief."

For four years, as an adolescent boy, he broods over his religion. He has drawn his knowledge of Christianity only from boyhood contacts with Unitarians. During his four years of meditation he admittedly speaks to no one on the matter. He makes no mention of reading the source material in the Bible. Then, with the accumulated wisdom of eighteen years, he renounces Christianity once and for all. Not only does he renounce it, but he becomes a bitter antagonist of Christianity. In what realm of human learning would a man be accepted as one entitled to speak with authority who had given to the subject only the uninformed, introverted, brooding consideration of a few boyhood years?

Julian Huxley (*Religion Without Revelation*, 1927) is more kindly disposed toward religion. He feels that the human heart demands religion and must have it. But he cannot stomach the musty theologies of the Church. Scientists within the Church " are filled with intellectual despair and long for a breath of the spirit of truth, which in the hands of science is transforming the world, to blow through their stuffy retreats." Here again we have a scientist judging Christianity entirely by what he has experienced in a very limited sphere of contacts and reading. He pronounces it extinct, but sees hope in the possibility that open-eyed scientists such as himself may be permitted to substitute a scientific humanism for the Christian Gospel. Naïvely he writes his book on religious questions, showing on every page an almost complete ignorance of what has been said and is being said on these questions by the great Christian thinkers, whose loyalty to the spirit of truth would not suffer in comparison with that of scientists.

Walter Lippmann, in his *Preface to Morals,* clears the ground for his new structure of morals by a sweeping indictment of Christianity. But, like those whom we have already considered, his knowledge of Christianity is that of the thoughtful man in the street and not that of the scientific investigator. He makes criticisms of Christianity as it exists today in our society, but criticisms with which in general many within the Church would agree. For him these criticisms prove the complete inadequacy of Christianity as a religion, but for us only the inadequacy of many of the existing forms of Christianity. There is no indication in his book that he has given a moment's thought to the question of the nature of Christianity according to the New Testament. It is striking that in all his estimations of Christianity he never once mentions the principle of love which in the New Testament is the center and heart of everything. That omission is sufficient evidence upon which to make the charge against Lippmann that he has dismissed Christianity without a hearing.

These, and others of similar mind and practice, are the prophets upon whose authority peculiarly Christian beliefs are considered an impossibility for intelligent modern men. If to be scientific means to investigate a subject thoroughly before pronouncing judgment, then in regard to religion these men have no right to speak as scientific thinkers. They are using their prestige in other fields of learning to lend them in the field of religion an authority to which they are not entitled. They have created an intellectual style in our time which coerces the human mind, which causes men to think they are being scientific when they wave aside Christian beliefs without due study and examination. There is something extremely childish in the assumed superiority of the gesture. It is reasonable to suspect that many, when, if ever, they grow out of the sophistication and become more open-minded, will be heartily ashamed of it.

The Place of Experience in Believing

We come back now to our original question, How can we believe? and we ask it, not in skepticism, but in a spirit of earnest inquiry. The Christian Gospel has made its appeal to us, creating in us the desire to put our entire life upon a thoroughly Christian basis. We know that this is possible only by our regulative beliefs and principles becoming thoroughly Christian. The question now arises, How can we know what the distinctive Christian beliefs and principles are, and how can we make them ours? What road must we take to find our way to a full and vital Christian faith? Where is our starting point?

An answer we often hear given is that we must start with the experience of salvation; that when a man is truly converted and brought into fellowship with God through Christ, he receives in his own heart the key which unlocks the mysteries of divine truth. What formerly seemed incredible to him now becomes acceptable and intelligible. There is a basic truth in this, but a truth that needs to be guarded carefully against error. It can easily be perverted into an excuse for the crassest obscurantism. Certainly it is in the nature of Christian truth that it cannot be grasped by the mind alone. Its meaning is not to be reached by the most earnest efforts of the speculative intellect. Looked at from the outside, it must seem a strange bundle of improbabilities. Christian teaching concerning the cross provides a good instance of this. The eye of the spectator sees a man, a Jewish religious teacher, suffering the misfortune of being executed as a common criminal. But the eye of faith sees in that death a revelation of the truth concerning life; men of faith confess that a strange redemptive power is mediated through the cross to them.

It is plain, then, that something has entered into their experience of which the mere spectator can know nothing, and that it is this which enables them to speak as they do about the cross. The spectator mind does not get through the outer shell of Christianity to its inner reality. There are many undoubtedly who think they

should be able to come to satisfactory conclusions concerning Christian beliefs upon a purely intellectual
basis. They desire to examine the subject from a safe
distance, and to decide from there what attitude they
must take in regard to it. Such persons can know nothing
of Christian truth. Truth, as Jesus used the term, is a
personal reality. It is never an abstract entity, but has
its content always in terms of human life. Truth and life
are inseparable. For a man to come to a knowledge of
the truth involves a transformation of the whole meaning and nature of life for him. The question of the nature of truth cannot be considered without opening up
the attendant question of the nature of life. To divorce
the two at any point is to create a rupture fatal to both.

The Biblical position may be stated briefly — that
there is no knowledge of Christian truth without commitment of life. He who desires to have all questions of
faith resolved and finally settled in his mind before he
comes to any decision in regard to the Christian life is
following a blind alley. He is adopting an attitude that
makes it impossible for him to see straight on any question of faith. Truth in Christianity always involves a
moral and spiritual decision, and evasion of the decision
issues necessarily in a blindness toward the truth.

This may explain to many why they have never been
able to make satisfactory progress in the understanding
of the Christian faith; why it has, in spite of their ef-

forts, remained a sealed book to them. They have expected to understand it and to unravel its problems in
much the same way as they would work through mathe-
matical or historical or even business problems, merely
by the exercise of their intellects. And yet because of its
very nature Christian truth refuses to unfold itself to
such investigation. The reality of it cannot be comprehended as truth unless at the same time it is received
and apprehended as life.

This is what is meant by saying that human reason is
helpless to search out the truth of the Gospel. There is
no mysticism or anti-intellectualism in this, no revolt
from reason. Rather an intensely practical spirit is here
at work, that practical spirit which is so dominant in
the New Testament. Christianity can never be an affair
of the mind alone. Its truth remains concealed from the
human reason until mind and heart and will are all
presented and respond to it with a single motion, in
thought, in feeling, and in action. There is no entrance
to the Kingdom of God except by way of repentance and
conversion, a turning round of the entire life to God.
Unwillingness to let the truth of the Gospel have its full
sway over heart and will shuts out the mind from all
real knowledge of it.

It seems, however, that every Christian truth has a
misinterpretation which follows it like a shadow and is
often mistaken for the truth itself. In this case the mis-

interpretation is that by religious experience we get on the inside of Christianity and arrive at its truth. In its crudest form this view makes enlightenment the product exclusively of a sudden conversion. We are told by some that we cannot understand anything of the true Gospel until we are soundly converted in accordance with their pattern.

This kind of conversion too often has, as a chief part of its content, an unquestioning acceptance of the religious standpoint and beliefs of the circle in which it takes place. A complete set of beliefs is adopted ready-made, and the convert then not only prides himself upon being one of the few enlightened, but considers himself competent to pronounce final judgment upon all matters of faith. He has arrived.

It is interesting to compare the spirit of such people with the spirit of Paul — Paul who, far on in life, said that he did not count himself to have apprehended. Strangely, conversion in New Testament times made men humble, conscious of their fallibility, and eager to be taught, but today conversion seems often to make men proudly assured, conscious of a kind of infallibility, and scornful of the possibility of being taught by any except those who will tell them merely what they already know.

There are various quarters from which we hear of the importance of religious experience. Earnest souls are drawn away from the Church to certain emotional and demonstrative religious groups because, they say, it gives them a definite Christian experience. Scientific theologians scrutinize the religious experience of the ages and devise for us ways and means of producing in the present what they call desirable forms of it. Ministers urge upon their people the necessity of having the great experiences of faith.

Surely the effect of all this emphasis is an unhealthy and futile straining after an inner experience which we do not possess. We feel that if we could attain to it we should have attained to faith; we should be believers. Sooner or later, however, we discover that even in religious experience we do not get beyond ourselves, that there may be no living God or living faith in this religion of human experience. It may be just a desperate attempt of the soul to lift its own spirituality up and set it on the throne of God. It may not lead us beyond ourselves, but in the last resort leave us alone with ourselves and without God.

Moreover, there is always this to be feared, that a man may have a highly emotional religious experience without having very much of what the prophets would be willing to call religion, a concern for justice, righteousness, and mercy in the affairs of everyday life. There are countless Christians who experience mystic raptures in worship whose religion ends pretty much with the end of the raptures. It is easy for religious experience thus to become the basis of a new kind of self-righteousness and Pharisaism.

We seem, then, to be in a dilemma. There is no believing worthy of the name without firsthand personal experience, and yet the fixing of our attention upon our own religious experience either in anticipation or in retrospect leads to an introverted and egocentric type of religiousness. Salvation is a great soul-enriching experience, the heights and depths of which no language can ever adequately express, but when men try to attain to such experience as a kind of steppingstone by means of which they shall ascend to God they are mistaking the fruits of faith for faith itself. That which comes first is, not an experience, but an act, an act of God in which God judges and man is judged, in which God pardons and man is pardoned, in which God redeems and man is redeemed. Our judgment, our pardon, our redemption, are a reality in the first place upon a far deeper level than our human experience; in fact, they are a reality before ever we are conscious of any experiences, for they have their primary existence in Jesus Christ. And though there may be many evidences of that reality in our experience, the basis of our assurance is, not what we have experienced, but what God has done and promises yet to do.

Believing Means Choosing

The question " How can we believe? " is asked usually with the idea in mind that what is desired and
needed is a change from a condition of not believing to
a condition of believing. But that assumes a totally false
view of our starting point. No man ever starts from
zero. We start from where we are in life and from the
beliefs and convictions which are already established in
us and are governing our existence. To ask, " How can
we believe? " is to ask the wrong question, for beliefs
of some kind about reality are inevitably present in us
whether we are conscious of them or not.

It happens often that men are unconscious of the real
beliefs which determine their conduct, deceiving themselves by holding a formal set of beliefs which are entirely divorced from relationship to conduct. The question which we should ask is, " Which belief shall be
ours? " Believing means choosing between two principles, between two kinds of life, between two gods, between self and God. Truth is never received as though
into a vacuum; it meets always with resistance from
within and sets us before a decision. A positive faith involves drastic negations. Our affirmations have no content unless they carry in them a rejection of what formerly we took to be the truth.

If this is so, more will be needed than to know what the Christian beliefs are and to be persuaded of the credibility of them. In some way we must come to a knowledge of the nature of our present beliefs and to the humbling recognition of wherein they are unchristian and ungodly.

If we are to believe, we must learn, not only the truth about God, but also the truth about ourselves. Merely accepting certain articles of religion as true is not belief. Believing is a passing from death to life, from falsehood to truth, from darkness to light. That cannot take place until it becomes clear to us wherein death rather than life possesses us. We cannot come to God unless we also come to ourselves. But it is just this that the revelation of God to which the Bible bears witness was able to do for men. Revelation in the Bible is never merely an unveiling of a Reality beyond life, but is always in the same moment an unveiling to man of the reality of his own heart and life. The vision of God is inseparable from the vision of self. When Isaiah in awe beholds the majesty and purity and holiness of God, immediately he is plunged into agony of soul by what the light of this revelation shows him concerning his own and his people's life. In the New Testament it is evident, especially in some of the parables, that for Jesus to bring a man to a knowledge of himself and to bring him to a knowledge of God was a single act. The two are inseparable. There is no knowledge of the truth about God without a corresponding knowledge of the truth about man.)

But this knowledge of God in which alone a man comes to a true knowledge of himself, cannot be described as it meets us in the Scriptures without using some such words as " reveal " and " revelation." Thus we are forced back farther and farther in our considerations until we have no alternative than to speak this word. Were our problem merely to demonstrate the reasonableness of Christian beliefs, there would be no need to talk of revelation. But our problem is how we may be freed from the domination of false beliefs into the liberty of the true faith. The light of reason proves itself a flickering candle in this darkness. False beliefs have always known how to use reason to establish themselves in man's esteem. It takes a more searching light to light up the darkness of our souls. The word which divides asunder as a sharp sword and discerns the thoughts and intentions of men is what is needed here — revelation.

In ourselves we have no starting point toward the truth. Such statements as have been made thus far might perhaps be regarded as rational deductions from experience. They are no such thing. They are convictions forced upon us by New Testament truth. What we have really been considering is, What, in the light of the New Testament, does it mean for a man to believe? Our presupposition all along has been the truth of the Gospel which already has met us and laid hold upon us. To stand aside objectively and judge from a neutral standpoint the matters under consideration is humanly impossible. No one is neutral on these questions. Let no man fool himself into thinking that he has examined religion objectively and thereby formed a detached judgment concerning it. Religion, being the question of human existence and of personality itself, is always examined from an established viewpoint. Why it should be more culpable for the viewpoint to be that of a believer in revelation than that of a believer in reason alone is hard to understand. Either may be regarded by the other as a prejudiced person.

Freedom to Believe Involves Freedom to Doubt

Christian belief is possible only as a response of man's mind, heart, and will to the truth which meets him in the Gospel. He is helpless to believe — he cannot believe — until the truth evidences itself to him as the truth for him and makes that kind of claim upon him which it is impossible for him to escape. The sacrilege of human compulsion in matters of belief is that it trespasses upon God's prerogative. It tries to do for a man what only God in his truth can do. There can be no compulsion except that which the truth contains in itself. A minister cannot induce right beliefs by exhortation, nor a parent by exerting parental pressure. Their only hope is that, in their words and lives, the truth of the Gospel may manifest itself and exert its own pressure.

A necessary corollary of this principle is the right to doubt. By some Christians, religious doubt is regarded as essentially sinful. They would be as shocked at the expression of a doubt as they would be at an unclean or blasphemous remark. Such an attitude is invariably the product of a shallow and unthinking faith. Doubts are the shadows cast by thought. They are the result of a soul's being dissatisfied with anything short of a personal apprehension of the truth; impatient of mere formal beliefs, but intensely concerned about the truth. Doubt must be respected when it is the mind of man holding fast to its integrity and refusing to bow in submission until forced by the truth itself to do so.

More of such doubt among Christians might be a forerunner of more vital Christian faith. We Christians need the fiercest blasts of skeptical criticism which are unloosed today to shake us free from our half-truths and our comfortable false certainties. In fact, it would be well if every religious teacher recognized that honest doubt usually means a soul open and eager for the truth. God shakes us out of *our* certainties that the way may be open for us to come to *his* certainties.

In the next chapter we shall have to consider the question of how God reveals his truth to us, the question of revelation. But we cannot escape the feeling that we have been going into our subject backward. That which we are to consider in the following chapters is in reality the basis of all that has been said in these opening chapters. Perhaps we should have begun boldly with the subject of revelation and the Scriptures, and considered afterward the importance and possibility of beliefs. Our justification for leaving the matter as it stands is that this is the order in which the subject seemed to open up. We were forced back and back upon revelation as our only place of beginning. No harm will be done so long as it is understood that, in the order of faith, revelation is always first and all else issues from it.

Chapter 3

The Word of God

THE CHURCH BELL rings out across the town announcing to all that something is about .o happen. That bell is a signal which is meant to awaken a peculiar expectation. We would not ring it for a lecture, even though the lecturer were the most distinguished on our continent. That it should be rung if some eminent statesman were about to speak on a subject of general interest would strike us at once as most incongruous. But when a service of Christian worship is soon to begin, the bell rings out boldly, summoning men from far and wide, and we feel that it is right that it should ring. It is evident that the expectation aroused has to do with something far greater than what the man who is to occupy the pulpit and conduct the service may say or do. If he thinks that the bells are ringing for *him* and because of the powers *he* is able to display, he is making a sad, egotistical mistake. The invitation of the bells is to come to *God's* house and in worship before *him* to hear the message which *He* would speak to us. The expectation with which we come, vague and inchoate though it may

be, is that somehow light may shine in upon our darkness — that revelation may actually take place.

The Centrality of the Bible in Our Churches

How that revelation takes place is the question before us in this chapter. The traditional answer of Protestantism, as all know, is that the Bible is the channel
of revelation. In some quarters that has been abandoned
in recent years as a wholly untenable position, and the
Bible is regarded as only one of the agencies of revelation. In other quarters the Bible has been endowed with
the attributes of God himself. The *channel* of revelation has been identified literally with the revelation. The
Bible on the pulpit has itself become an object of worship instead of merely the agency by which we come to
the Object of all true worship. This question of the
true place of the Bible is an issue of primary importance
in Protestantism today, and the decision we make in regard to it will determine many other decisions.

Whatever view in reality prevails, in form, at least,
the Bible still maintains its central place in Protestant
worship. It is the only book that rests there upon the
pulpit before the eyes of all. The readings are from it,
and the psalms and hymns are to a large extent para-
phrases of parts of it or free renderings of thoughts
from it. Few ministers would begin their sermon with-

out announcing a Biblical text, although in some cases that may be the last that is heard of the text. Formally, in our worship the Bible is still accorded pre-eminence. But this is hardly honest unless we still hold to the conviction responsible originally for such pre-eminence. If the Bible is not entitled to that solitary position in worship, then it must be removed. It may be worth inquiring first into the reasons that impelled men to place it in that position, keeping our minds open the while to the possibility that those reasons may still hold good.

The Reformation, which resulted in the formation of our Protestant Churches, did not begin, as so many seem to think, with a protest against the abuses and corruptions of the old Catholic Church, but with a new understanding of the message of the Bible. Here and there a few men, quietly reading the Scriptures and delving into them in earnest, discovered a message the like of which they themselves had never heard before, a message of which the highest dignitaries of the Church and the most learned scholars seem to have had no knowledge. A truth which carried its own authority met them in the Scriptures and by the sheer force of its truthfulness overpowered them and took them wholly captive. They were held by it as in a vise and could not and would not set themselves free. It transformed their personal lives and remolded their entire spiritual outlook. It gave them firm convictions as to what Christianity and the Church must be in order to be true to their own natures. Then, in the Church, at first very quietly, later more vigorously, these men began to raise a protest *for* this truth. This positive use of the word " protest," which an examination of the etymology of the word shows to be the original one, has slipped out of common use, leaving the negative sense of a protest *against* something as the dominant meaning. But with the Reformers, the negative protest against the errors and corruptions of the Church was only secondary, arising of necessity from this primary *testimony for* the rediscovered Gospel.

At first the Reformers had no intention of breaking away from the Church of their fathers or of founding a new Church. Their one concern was for the truth of the Gospel, and their one desire was that the whole Church in all its life might be brought into the fullest harmony with that Gospel. It was not until the Church refused to let itself be changed in any way, until the *official* Church condemned as false the Gospel which was life to these men and commanded them to give up their beliefs, that they were forced to move out of the old Church and to found a new one. With Martin Luther they had to say: " Here I stand. I cannot do otherwise. So help me God." The truth for them was not a formal creed which they held in their minds and

could change at will. The truth held them and possessed
them so that they were no longer free. They could not
change from it even at the command of the mightiest
lords of Church and State. In loyalty to the Scriptures
they had to let themselves be driven out of the Church
because they could not acknowledge the authority of
an external Church to be superior to the authority of
the truth of the Word of God.

It is not difficult, therefore, to see why the original
Protestant Churches gave such a pre-eminent place to
the Scriptures, and centered their worship upon the reading and exposition of them. It was the message of the
Scriptures that had brought about the formation of their
Churches, and, naturally, they were convinced that an
understanding of that message was the first essential
for their preservation and growth.

But we have not yet touched the point that indicates
the full significance of the Bible in Protestant worship
and life. The place given the Bible is not to be understood from an examination of the qualities of its individual books, however excellent they may be. It does
not owe its title, " The Book," to a superiority over all
other literature which can be made evident by comparison. It was the knowledge that something happens
through the instrumentality of this Book, which happens through no other book, that caused it to be set
apart. Its unique claim is that in it God speaks to man

and God comes to man; his Word is made flesh; light shines in darkness.

The peculiarly Protestant claim is that it is through " The Word," and through it alone, that God makes himself known to man. One hears Protestants speak scoffingly of the Roman Catholic doctrine of the Real Presence in the Sacrament, as though that were a flagrant superstition. But how many of them know anything of a Protestant doctrine of the Real Presence? The claim is nothing more or less than this — that God's actual presence becomes known through the word of the Scriptures. The expectation of the Roman Catholic worshiper is that in the mystic act of the Sacrament God will come to him. The expectation of the Protestant worshiper should be that, as he waits in faith before the word of the Scriptures, God himself will come to him and speak to him the message which he needs to hear.

All preaching must be ordered in the light of this divine possibility. When the preacher uses the pulpit as a rostrum for the propagation of his views of life and of things in general, when his personality pushes into the forefront and engages the attention, when it becomes hard for the worshiper to look beyond the preacher, the central purpose of Protestant worship is completely lost. The powerlessness and emptiness of much of our worship results from the fact that by ministers and worshipers alike the divine possibility, that God himself should come to us and speak to us, has been forgotten. It makes a vast difference in one's preparation of a sermon whether one expects merely to talk to people *about* God or to deliver a message which may be the medium through which the Eternal God himself will speak to man.

This latter sets before us the audacious claim which Protestantism makes for preaching. The proclamation of the message of the Scriptures is central in Reformed worship because in it God ceases to be the One who is spoken about and becomes the One who speaks. The word which sounded forth into life in the prophets and apostles, and in Jesus, with life-transforming power, and which men apprehended as God himself speaking, can sound forth with the same power today. But it must be the word that came through the prophets and apostles and in Jesus. It must be the same word come alive again, or it will not be the word of God. For that reason it is the Bible alone that rests upon the pulpit and is the source of the message in our worship.

Neglect of the Bible Today

When we look into the life of the Church today, one of the first observations we make is that the Bible has fallen into disuse. There may be more copies of it sold each year than of any other book, but that does not mean that it is read. Anyone may with ease verify the statement that few Church members study their Bibles today.

It is a serious indictment against our Sunday Schools that the period of their rise and expansion has seen a steady decline *among Christians* of interest in and knowledge of the Bible. There is a causal relationship between the two phenomena. The Sunday School has been permitted to displace the home as the center of religious instruction. Parents feel that they are fulfilling their vow " to teach their children the truths and duties of the Christian faith " when they merely send them to Sunday School. As a result, children get a scrappy half hour of teaching once each week when even fifteen minutes each day at home would mean nearly two hours of instruction in the week. Also the Sunday School quarterlies have, in countless instances, helped to promote the disuse of the Bible. Put a Bible into the hands of a boy who for years has used only a quarterly and it will be a strange book to him. How many persons are there who, after ten to fifteen years in Sunday School, have a working knowledge of the Bible, who know their way through its paths, and who have found that in it which will keep them searching its pages as long as they live?

It is disastrous that Sunday Schools have gone beyond their original intention of ministering to children whose parents were incompetent to instruct them. Both for parents and for children it has resulted in the Bible's becoming a closed book. Let Christian parents be warned — if they do not lead their children into a love of the Scriptures and an understanding of its truths, they are neglecting their first Christian duty to those children and are starting them in life with a most serious spiritual handicap. That duty dare not be left to Sunday Schools or any other agencies. A secondary effect of the disappearance of religious instruction from the home is that the parent ceases to be a student of the Bible. Nothing teaches like teaching. It is not until we endeavor to impart knowledge to others that we realize the insufficiency of our own understanding. Parents who undertake to teach their children will become acutely conscious of their own need to be instructed and will come seeking help from the Church.

Another factor that has encouraged the disuse of the Bible has been the growing popular consciousness of the discrepancy between the traditional interpretations of the Bible and the critical interpretations at which modern scholarship has arrived. Many a Christian has come to feel that the Bible raises problems with which he is not competent to deal. He is unable to accept the old, traditional, literalistic views, but he is afraid that the new views will carry him to a radical position in which he can hardly claim any longer to be a Christian. The idea persists that to be a Christian one must believe, literally, that the whale swallowed Jonah, and that the entire Creation was completed in six days of twenty-four hours each. There has also been a general impression that modern scholarship has discredited the Bible and thrown most of it into the discard.

That these impressions and ideas have remained in the minds of men is the guilt of the Christian ministry. Far too often ministers have been afraid to deal with the literary problems of the Scriptures with frankness, and thus have permitted their intelligent parishioners to be turned away from the Scriptures by things which seem to them insuperable obstacles. It is a shame, for the effect of what scholars have done in the last hundred years in the scientific study of the Scriptures should be to make them far more interesting and fascinating than they have ever been.

The integrity of the Bible's message is not shaken at any point. Rather, at a thousand points, preliminary obstacles are cleared away to leave an open path for the message to come to us. When we get clearly in our minds that the first chapter of Genesis is not meant to be a final pronouncement upon either geography or cosmography, and therefore that it has no quarrel with the scientific investigation of the origin of the universe, we are at the point where that chapter can speak to us of a God who was and is Creator of all things. When we get the book of Jonah disengaged from the problem of whether or not a fish might swallow a man and after three days vomit him forth alive, and when we understand the setting in which the story of Jonah was told, we marvel that the incisive missionary message of this book remains unknown to so many Christians. We need have no fears that the scientific investigation of the Scriptures will rob us of our Bible. It may make us change our understanding of its structure at many points, but the sum effect should be to open wide the Bible before us and to draw our minds away from unessential puzzles to the essential message. It is the Church's lack of courage and frankness in dealing with problems raised by these new investigations that has caused men to turn away from the Scriptures.

Another source of present-day ignorance of the Bible is the dearth of expository preaching. Preaching has tended more and more to become purely topical. The minister takes a subject from the field of religion or morals which interests him, and gives to his people his opinions and convictions on that subject, hanging them if possible on the hook of a Scripture text. The question has become, " What will interest these people? " rather than, " What is the message which, as a Christian minister, I must preach to these people whether they wish to hear it or not? " It is forgotten that the word " minister " is a shortened form of the old name " minister of the Word." The minister becomes the man of spiritual attainments and interests, with a plausible philosophy of life, who seeks to transmit these to his people for their benefit. He is thus a minister of his own excellences rather than the minister of a message that will always be beyond him as well as beyond his people.

The task of a minister of the Word is humbler, and less fearful for him who is confident neither of his own spiritual attainments nor of the sufficiency of his philosophy of life. He comes week by week to the Scriptures, seeking to hear a message that is needed in his own life and in the life of his people. The fact of his own poverty of spirit does not turn him aside from the ministry, but joins him all the closer to his people in waiting for the light to break forth from the Word and shine in upon their darkness. He speaks, not as one who *has* the revelation and is able with competency to pass it on to others. He speaks rather as one who knows where the revelation is to be found and seeks ever afresh to bring his people, and himself with them, to the point where the light of revelation will flash forth. It will be admitted that there is not much expository preaching *of that kind* in the Churches.

Thus, for a variety of reasons, the Bible has fallen into the background. And we shall not make any mistake in setting this in direct relationship with the prevailing uncertainty of mind among Christians regarding their beliefs. Ignorance of the Bible must inevitably result in ignorance of the fundamentals of Christian faith. The Bible presents to us the sources from which alone we can gain a firsthand knowledge of the faith in which we stand. Neglect of it makes it necessary for us to depend for our knowledge upon what we are told. But human transmission inevitably distorts the truth and creates misconceptions. We need constantly to be going back to the source, that we may draw pure, fresh water for ourselves. It seems evident that there is little hope of Christians' making any headway toward definite convictions and vital beliefs until they, and the Church with them, get the Bible open again and restore it to the center of the Christian life.

General Versus Specific Revelation

Tracing the steps by which the Bible fell into neglect, however, does not give us any adequate reason for this neglect. The really determining factor lies much deeper. That which is ultimately responsible is the conception of revelation that has become widely prevalent, not only in religious thought that makes itself vocal, but, more seriously, in the *unconscious* religious attitude of vast numbers of people. This idea is that God reveals himself everywhere and in all things. Turn to nature and you will find him there. Look up to the starry sky or inward upon the human conscience and you behold the majesty of God. Search through the best literature of any nation, read the history of man, listen to the finest music, and in all of these God will speak to you. The whole creation is, as Carlyle puts it, the visible garment of the invisible God. Then to this is added that God speaks to man in the Scriptures of the Old and New Testaments. Some insist upon a particular emphasis on the Scriptures, write revelation with a large R, but that is all. This, or some slight variant of it, is the view of revelation most widely held, not only in the Protestant Churches, but by men in general today. It meets us in literature, in sermons, in conversation, and even in some more recently written Church creeds. It is the presupposition of many religious writings; and it is so generally assumed to be the only intelligent attitude possible that we hesitate to disagree.

Upon principle, however, we must disagree. It is not an obscurantist view to claim an exclusive revelation in the Scriptures. A *different* view of revelation, indeed, it is, and certainly one that at first sight offends the mind of the average educated man of today. Even so, there is no reason a priori for pronouncing it unintelligent and narrow. No such judgment is passed upon the scientist for saying that in chemistry certain knowledge can be arrived at only by a prescribed series of experiments. He is not a bigot for asserting that such knowledge is not to be gained either by gazing at the stars or by studying art. Nor would he be accused of lack of appreciation of nature or of art. Why, then, should it be regarded as a sign of narrowness to assert that the field of revelation is the Scriptures? If in the order of things it is through them that God reveals himself, it is so, and we have no more reason to quarrel with this assertion than to quarrel with a chemist who says that a particular truth should be accessible only by certain experiments. The primary religious issue today is between these two conceptions of revelation: that God reveals himself in all things or that God reveals himself through the Scriptures.

The general view of revelation is mainly responsible for neglect of the Bible. If God speaks to us everywhere, then a knowledge of the Scriptures can no longer be considered indispensable. It may be urged as desirable for the attainment of the highest excellence, but on a moderate plane of virtue one can get on tolerably well without it. Few are likely to undertake serious study of their Bibles when it is much simpler and less onerous to listen for the voice of God elsewhere. They are content with conscience and nature.

That there are spiritual voices all about us none but the blindest and most callous fool would deny. Nature provides rich joys for us and can purify and uplift us. Conscience is our constant guide. Through literature we feed our minds upon the thoughts of great men. History instructs us. We do not close our ears to any of the voices which sound from every quarter of human life.

But we do say that in the Scriptures there comes to us a revelation of God which does not come in any other way. We hear a voice which, once we have heard it, is not to be confused with any of the spiritual voices we hear elsewhere. It alone speaks to us of a sovereign God who is Father of our spirits, of a Redeemer who is God incarnate, of a Spirit which is the Spirit of that Father and that Redeemer actually alive and at work in man today, of a Church of men which becomes the very body of the Redeemer, of the forgiveness of sins which is the transformation of man into the likeness of Christ, and of the life everlasting which is the perfecting of the new creation. It is senseless to claim that *this* revelation is made everywhere and in all things.

The mistake has been that the word "revelation" has been used carelessly of all truth. Thus this general conception has been permitted to displace the peculiarly Christian conception of *the* Truth, which is the redemption and the reconciliation of the whole of life to God. Men are reluctant to admit that revelation is confined to the Scriptures, having the feeling that thereby they would be turning their backs upon the truths which are being unveiled constantly in every sphere of human life. The fear is without grounds; we are not closing our minds against truth, from whatever quarter it may come. But when we give to revelation the general and not the Christian sense, we introduce hopeless confusion. We can never set the Voice and the voices in proper order so that we can tell where our loyalty is demanded. There remains also the possibility that the voice we choose to obey may be only an objectification of our own desires. Life provides a confusion of voices. The authority of the Scriptures is that there sounds forth from them a single Voice, completely consistent in its demands and its promises, manifesting from beginning to end one purpose and one will, and evidencing itself to the mind and heart and conscience of man as the voice of God.

We may illustrate the practical importance of a man's view of revelation by referring to recent events in the Church in Germany. That God speaks in history has become a commonplace of religious thought. What is meant is not merely that we may learn valuable lessons from the study of history, but that in all history God reveals himself, so that a man of discernment should be able thereby to arrive in some degree at a knowledge of God's will. During the first year of the Nazi regime in Germany, a section of the Protestant Church began to apply this principle with full earnestness in a way that seemed to them perfectly legitimate. They were convinced that God had spoken to them in the events of

German history in the early months of 1933. In their
enthusiasm for the national resurrection they felt called
to take up the task of reconstructing and revitalizing the
German Church. The sorry record of these followers
of Bishop Müller, who took the name " German Christians," makes it hard for us to grasp the essential sincerity of many of them, at least in the beginning. Undoubtedly they heard a voice, which they had been
taught to interpret as the voice of God himself, com-
manding them to transform the Church. History had
spoken. They were caught up in a great spiritual enthusiasm for what seemed the task of the hour. But when
we learn that by purification of the Church they meant
the cleansing from it of all non-Aryans and a reconstruction of it that would make it fit into the new Nazi
order, we are disposed to say that it was not God, but
rather a demon of some kind, that spoke to them in history. History seems to have a way of saying what man
wants it to say, and so is likely to do no more than echo
back in authoritative form human pride and purposes
and passions.

The common deification of conscience is an equally
illuminating example. The general idea is that man has
a natural faculty for discriminating between right and
wrong. " Let conscience be your guide," is given as an
all-sufficient maxim for the moral life. But unfortunately
conscience proves a poor divinity. It has been known to

command cruelties and to drive men into the most perverted actions. Some of the greatest wrongs of all time have been committed at the bidding of conscience. Certainly those who put Jesus to death were conscientious men.

Then, again, who has not had the distressing experience of listening for the guidance of the inner voice and hearing nothing? That experience results often in despair, especially in young persons; they feel themselves spiritual monstrosities because their consciences do not speak out with such plainness as older people tell them should be the case. The despair disappears only when one realizes that it is in the nature of conscience that uninstructed it cannot speak.

The worst result, however, of regarding conscience as a sufficient source for knowing the will of God is that it inevitably lowers the standard of Christian living. The conscience of the individual is formed by the influences that surround him from earliest years on. The standard of life it demands will be determined by the nature of those influences. By calling conscience the voice of God, one substitutes this standard of life for Christ, who alone should be the standard of Christian living. Not Christ, but conscience, becomes man's guide. And the result, as we see it all about us, is that Christian living is reduced to a level of dull respectability. The appeal of really Christlike living ceases to be felt.

Peculiarly Christian standards become "counsels of perfection," and the average Christian is content if he can fulfill the more moderate demands of his own conscience. The peace of a good conscience which many enjoy is not the peace of reconciliation with the God of the prophets and the Father of Jesus Christ, but the false and deadly peace of an easier reconciliation with the demands of their own social environment.

There is reason to suspect, then, that whenever a second source of revelation is tolerated alongside the Scriptures, the result is confusion. It becomes a second god, and the God of the Scriptures fades into the background. The real authority over life is wielded, not by Him but by the rival god. The acceptance of a general revelation by a Christian is thus in essence a dividing of his loyalty, which is disloyalty to his God.

The Fathers of the Church knew what they were doing when they fenced off the Scriptures from all other writings and defined the canon as the field of revelation. They did it, not because of the particular qualities and characteristics of the several books, but because they heard a voice there which they were assured was to be heard in its purity nowhere else. But, say some, are we to believe that God's glorious revelation of himself is bound up between the two covers of a book? The revelation is not bound; it fills all creation and has to do with every detail of human life, for all things are of

God. But the records of God's self-revelation, through which alone we are able to know him as the Creator, Redeemer, and Reconciler of all life, are contained between the two covers of a book, and, if we are too proud to seek him where he has chosen to make himself known, then we must remain in ignorance of him. Who are we to dictate how God shall reveal himself? If God has chosen to speak his word to us through the instrumentality of persons and events within the history of the Jews, and if the records of that revelation are gathered in the form of a book, why should we find that strange or unbelievable? Our part here as everywhere in life is simply to seek the truth where it is to be found.

The Scriptures and Revelation Are Not Identical

The Scriptures are the field in which the light of revelation shines forth. But the Scriptures and the revelation are not to be identified as though they were letter by letter the same. Most of those who in recent years have stood out for the primacy of the Scriptures have made the mistake of this literal identification. They have tried to maintain the infallibility of the Bible as a whole, instead of the infallibility of the message God speaks to us in the Bible. This literalism, on the one hand, blocks open-minded investigation of the Scrip-

tures and drives faith into an obscurantist position, and,
on the other hand, makes " the word of God " mean
something vastly different from what it plainly means
in the pages of Scripture. " The word of God," for the
prophets, was God's will for his people, expressed either
in speech or in symbolic actions. In the Second Isaiah,
" the word of God " signifies the plans and purposes
which God is working out in human history and which
he has made known through his prophets; it is the
knowledge of himself and of his will which he has set
in the heart and mind of Israel as a sacred trust for the
world. In the New Testament, Jesus says in the parable
of the Sower, " The seed is the word of God." That
seed cannot by any stretch of imagination be identified
literally with the words of a book. It is the truth of God
which, when sown in men's lives, grows up and gradually ripens into a great harvest. In the Gospel of John
Jesus himself is called the Word of God. The Word,
then, is a living Person. The Word of God is not a book,
but a divine Reality, with which we come into contact
today only through the records of a book. Martin
Luther said that the Bible is the cradle in which the
Word of God is laid. It is the same thing to say that it is
the temple into which we must enter reverently if we
would hear what God would speak to us. If Christian
people would keep this distinction in mind, it would save
them from much confusion and needless puzzlement,

and it would set the Word free to be heard in its purity.

In this Word, then, the truth, which is not just the truth about God or about life, but which *is* God and life, comes to us. Faith is the hearing of this Word, the joyful receiving of it as our life, and the giving of ourselves in patient obedience as it marks out for us our way step by step through life. But when we try to say *how* the Word comes to us and what it means when it does come, we have to speak of God the Father Almighty, of Jesus Christ, his Son, of the Holy Spirit, of the Church, of the forgiveness of sins, and of the life everlasting. The entire creed is an attempt to comprehend the Word which God speaks to us for our salvation.

Chapter 4

God the Father Almighty

A THOUGHTFUL LAYMAN was commenting upon a series of sermons preached by his minister on the central Christian doctrines. " He began," he said, " with the doctrine of God, and it was a very good sermon, but I suspect that neither he nor we were much the wiser concerning God when he finished than when he began." It is hard to keep from being a little cynical whenever we hear anyone attempt to speak definitely of God, especially if the attempt be professedly to explain this matter of God and make it clear.

The trouble is that we talk of God as though he were a problem in economics, or a specimen to be dissected. We discuss God, completely forgetful that what this God thinks of us is vastly more important than what we think of him. When we hear certain opinionated individuals pronouncing, " Now this is what *I* think of God," it is hard to resist asking, " But have you considered as yet what God may think of you? " The beginning of all knowledge of God is the fear of God, the bowing down of man's soul in deepest reverence before the mystery of the Eternal. Where such reverence dwells, there will be no misapprehensions concerning the puny words in which we undertake to speak of God. They will be recognized as what they are — half-blind gropings to comprehend the Ultimate Reality of life. The man who speaks of God with an air of assurance and easy familiarity betrays thereby only his ignorance of what he professes to know. God is not subject to our definitions. God is far beyond all our knowing and comprehending. We catch but glimpses of him. The Infinite is not to be comprehended by the finite.

We could put the same thing in this way, that in our knowledge of God we are always having to go back and begin again with the A B C's. Usually when we have learned the elements of a subject, we are able from that time forward to take them for granted and pass on to higher knowledge. In regard to God we never reach the stage where we can take even the simplest elements of knowledge for granted. Again and again we have to return to the spiritual kindergarten and spell out afresh the A B C's of faith. Perhaps that was part of Jesus' meaning when he said that we must become as little children if we would enter into the Kingdom.

The Trinity

The first characteristic of our Christian belief in God is expressed in the doctrine of the Trinity. Although we are monotheists and believe in one God alone, we confess our faith in God as Father, Son, and Holy Spirit. To many people that statement is arrant nonsense, the babbling of persons who cannot, or will not, discern the difference between one and three. Perhaps a large percentage of Christian people would have to admit that for them the Trinity is a metaphysical puzzle which they have long since given up trying to solve. They regard it as one of those mysterious and incomprehensible things which they must accept in order to be full-fledged Christians but which make little or no practical difference in life. Invariably the trouble is that men approach the doctrine of the Trinity as though it were a problem in arithmetic. They think of it in terms of numbers, and therefore find in it only darkness and confusion. We ought rather to think of it as the form of expression which the early Christians were forced to use by the nature of the Reality which they sought to describe. They could not state what God meant to them in any other form than that of the Trinity.

From of old the Israelite forefathers had conceived God as the Creator of all things, the Lord of heaven and earth, a God of righteousness but also of mercy. The persistent faith of Israel, which alone preserved the nation from dissolution, was this confidence in a beneficent overruling power. The nation might be shattered, but even its ruin could be used by God in the working out of his purpose. However disastrous the

events of the outer world might be, however dark and
hopeless the outlook upon life might be, there was always a remnant in Israel that refused to surrender the
outward course of life to chaos and blind fates. This
faith in a God who is the Father Almighty was bound
to be taken up and have new light shed upon it in the
Christian society. The disciples could see with clearness
that it was Jesus' own faith in God.

Then, as the disciples sought to put in words what
Jesus had meant and was meaning to them, they could
find no adequate word except this word " God." They
were fully conscious of what a seemingly unbelievable
claim they were making, and of the ridicule it would be
certain to call forth. Forced, nevertheless, by the reality that had met them in Jesus, they made the claim.
Through Jesus of Nazareth and all his influence upon
them, something had happened to them which made
them certain he was none other than the Christ of God.
To tell the whole truth about Jesus as it was known to
them, they *had* to say that God was in him, both in the
terribleness of his judgment and in the marvelousness
of his mercy.

But even then they had not said all. There was an
indwelling Presence, a Power not their own, which
Christians experienced as the actual Presence and Power
of God working in them. It was the Spirit of God the
Father and at the same time it was the Spirit of Jesus

Christ. An exalted spiritual mood or a mystic experience of the soul was not adequate to explain this experience. A Spirit for which man's spirit formed only the temple had come upon them. It meant an actual fellowship with God in daily life and an opening up of undreamed-of spiritual resources.

These three realities, which were nevertheless a single personal reality in their nature, had to be given their full import when the Christian tried to say what God meant to him. There was no intention of creating a philosophical puzzle to perplex the minds of future generations. Nor was this doctrine of the Trinity propounded by theologians as a sacred mystery to be understood by the learned few. It was meant originally to be, and it ought still to be, a simple statement of the reality of God in the ordinary Christian's life. The man who dismisses the Trinity as an antiquated theological form is dismissing the Christian God, and with him the peculiarly Christian life. This doctrine is of the utmost practical significance. We cannot enter into the meaning of life as it was revealed to the early Christians except as we enter into the full meaning of God as he was revealed to them — Father, Son, and Holy Spirit, a threefold reality. And when we have found God so that we can say all three of these words with sincerity, we know, as the early Christians did, that it is one God in all three who meets us and possesses our lives.

Faith in God

The first distinction in regard to our belief in God concerning which we must be clear is that it is not faith that there is a God, but faith in God, which occupies our attention. There is a real difference. The first is hardly more than a tenacious opinion, a mental acceptance of the possibility of a Deity, not involving one's personal existence in any essential manner. The second, wherever we see it in the Scriptures, means entering into a personal relationship with God that affects the remotest details of one's life. What many people call their faith in God betrays itself at once as the false article by the fact that it makes little or no difference in their daily lives. It is a religious appendage, which might be removed without any very serious disturbance to their lives other than the immediate pain of the operation. They do not live by it. They carry it with them, often feeling it as a bit of a burden; it does not carry them. The test of the reality of a man's faith in God is the difference it makes in the form and content of his daily life. It may humble us to examine ourselves and find to what extent that which we have counted our faith in God is just a vague but comforting and reassuring conviction that somewhere and somehow there is a God.

The Bible has little to say in praise of belief that

there is a God. In fact, the prophets said some very bitter things about people who plainly counted themselves believers, in this sense of the word, even though they worshiped the God of Israel with diligence. The prophets knew that a pious acceptance of the fact of God might mean nothing at all, and might be used to provide peace and reassurance of soul without any response to God's demands. It is with reason that the Bible contains no proofs of the existence of God. The men of the Bible were not interested in that question; they passed it by deliberately, because it did not lead in the direction in which they desired to go. They knew that to prove to a man that there is a God, even if the proof is effective, is more likely to result in a sterile mental assurance of God than in a definite commitment of life to Him.

Most discussion today concerning God is on this lower plane — is there a God? Atheists and agnostics are busy setting forth proof, which to them is conclusive, that God is an unnecessary hypothesis, that the man of intelligence can understand the universe and live a worth-while life best without the encumbrance of a Deity. When people speak of their faith being taken from them or of casting off their faith, it is usually this objective faith in the existence of a personal God that they have lost. Had their faith been of the kind the Bible sets before us as faith in God, a personal commitment of life, it would have taken more than rational arguments to shake it. From the side of the Church also the discussion concerning God is often kept on this lower fruitless plane. Argument after argument, sometimes plausible, sometimes specious, is conjured up in order to prove that there must be a God.

A recent writer says that the most acute religious problem of this generation, especially for young people, centers at this point. The work of Thomas Huxley, and of those who followed in his tradition, has created wave after wave of unbelief, which has affected, not only the intellectuals, but, by indirect influence, many who have never even heard the name of Huxley. How should one meet this unbelief? Should he thank God that newer and more up-to-date scientists are offering pronouncements favorable to a spiritual view of the universe? What a relief that scientists are going to let us believe in a God after all! They bowed him out of the universe, and we wept; they bow him back in, and from the Church Universal there goes up a deafening shout of welcome and thanksgiving. Surely something is wrong. What must the world think of a Church which sets such store by the dictum of science? The Church would be far wiser to follow the example of the Bible and refuse to be interested in this question of the existence of God. Going down and arguing upon that plane, we are vulnerable at once, for it is in the nature of Christian truth that it cannot be established by rational proof. And even when we have done our utmost and have convinced someone that there is a God, that assurance may work, not for the glory of God and the salvation of man, but for the creation of a sterile certainty and false security.

The question concerning God with which the Bible always makes its beginning is, " Which God will you choose? " Moses receives the commandment, " Thou shalt have no other gods before me." Elijah on Mount Carmel cries: " How long halt ye between two opinions? if the Lord be God, follow him: but if Baal, then follow him." Jesus says, " Ye cannot serve God and mammon." The assumption is that a man worships and devotes himself to something, some power, some element in life. His god may be the human reason, or material power, or money, or alcohol, or his nation, or, commonest of all, himself. But there is always something to which man gives the supreme place in life; he cannot avoid it. Thus, the Bible does not set before us the alternative of God or no God, but rather it sets us before the decision whether the gods we have made for ourselves, and are continually making, are worthier of our worship and life's devotion than the God of the prophets and apostles and of Jesus. Belief in God is not assent to a hypothesis concerning the universe, but rather a choosing between alternatives in actual life.

The God-Centeredness of Faith

There has been a tendency in recent years to think of faith almost entirely in terms of human experience. Faith in God is described as a great religious experience into which we may enter. It is something *within* us which today may be at high tide and tomorrow at low ebb. We examine and analyze it, perhaps with the aid of psychology, in the great souls of Biblical and Christian history, and we try to emulate it in ourselves. We cultivate the mystic moods of our souls, feeling that in them we can draw closest to these great experiences of faith. In all this the eyes are turned inward and the chief interest of religion is centered upon inducing and maintaining in oneself, and perhaps in others, an attitude of soul which is called faith.

The men of faith, the outpourings of whose souls we read in the Bible, had certainly a richness of inner experience, but never do we find them putting the center of things in such experience. The center for them is never in anything human, but ever in the eternal and abiding God. The strength of their faith is no strength residing in themselves, but just the firmness of the hand of God which holds them in life. They are not introspective, trying to work themselves into an attitude or mood of faith, but rather the opposite. They look away from themselves, away from even the best and highest and most spiritual that they might find in themselves, and seek all their help from One whom they call the Living God.

Eduard Thurneysen, theologian and first preacher in the Cathedral of Basle, Switzerland, states that he finds those who come to him for spiritual help always concerned about something wrong in their religious attitude and their relationship to God. Something has gone crooked in their spiritual experience, and they want help to put it straight again. The only answer he can give them is that they had best turn their eyes away from their spiritual experience and their relationship to God. In the nature of things their experience will always be, it *must* always be, broken, imperfect, unsatisfying. Looking in upon ourselves we ought never to find other than that. Conflict, uncertainty, insecurity, entanglement, sin — that is the true nature of our human life, if we have eyes to see it. We have to begin with God's relationship to us if we would find something upon which we can lean all our weight. Our redemption is not dependent upon our varying spiritual moods, but upon One who through all our moods and experiences is working out his purpose of love. It is what *God* is that forms the ground of our hope, our confidence, and our peace.

Repentance and Obedience

How can we know this God whom to know is life?
We long for a faith that will keep us always strong, or
at least will provide us with a daily refreshing of our
strength, that we may run and not be weary, that we
may walk and not faint. With the psalmist, we want to
have God as our refuge and strong tower, a shelter
from every bitter wind. When we ask the prophets and
psalmists and Evangelists to tell us the way to such faith
as was theirs, they give us no reasonable instructions.
They show us no road to follow that we may arrive at
the desired destination. Instead, they confront us with
the blunt ultimatum: " Repent." Consistently from beginning to end the Bible affirms that there is no other
way to God than this — repentance, a turning round of
man in his spirit and in his life. The abruptness of Jesus
with Nicodemus in demanding of him that he should be
born again when the good man came politely offering to
discuss points of religion has often been noted. That
abruptness is characteristic of the whole Bible. We come
to it like Nicodemus, politely interested in religion, de-
siring to improve our faith, only to meet at every point
this embarrassing and pointed assertion that the obstacle to faith is in our own natures, and that there must
be a radical change in us if we are to know God.

Whether it is called repentance, or rebirth, or the taking away of blindness from the eyes, or the giving of a new heart, it is all the same thing. There is no way to belief in God that does not involve the transformation through God's Spirit of one's heart and life.

Here we reach the place where our human helplessness becomes most apparent. We cannot repent; we cannot change ourselves or give ourselves new hearts. We are up against a blank wall. That is just the place to which we have to come, or, rather, where we have to see that we *always are,* before there is any help for us. It is there that our human pride becomes completely broken, and in the nakedness of our need we reach out empty imploring hands to God. We wait for the Lord with an urgency in our waiting like those that watch for the morning. We become " the poor in spirit." Then our God in his mercy comes to us, and fills our empty hands, and by giving us himself gives us all we need. He creates in us a clean heart and renews a right spirit within us. He opens a door for us in the blank wall and takes us into his Kingdom. It is then that we can say, with our whole souls, and with an assurance which nothing can shake, that we believe in God the Father.

If faith in God begins in repentance, it has its continuance in obedience. Perhaps we are not accustomed to hearing these two words, faith and obedience, spoken in one breath, but the falsity of much that we call our

faith is that it has no obedience in it. Faith without obedience is like a spirit without a body; it cannot exist in
this world. Repentance is always a call to relinquish
one's own will and purposes in life and to accept God's
will and purposes. The form in which the prophets put
the demand was, " Choose ye whom ye will serve." The
content of repentance or rebirth is an acceptance of
God's will, and the content of a life of faith is obedience
to that will step by step. The fullness and richness and
joyfulness of our faith is determined directly by the completeness of our obedience. Our obedience is not a fulfillment of the Law in our own strength. Rather, it is the
fruit of the Spirit. God's Spirit makes us open and sensitive to his commands and eager to respond to them, and
we see in them, not burdens being laid upon us, but our
life's truest opportunities being opened before us. There
is no such thing as a believing in God which is not also
an obedience to him in love.

The Sovereignty of God

The Apostles' Creed speaks of " God the Father
Almighty, Maker of heaven and earth." The great
prophet-evangelist calls him " the everlasting God, the
Lord, the Creator of the ends of the earth." It is here
that many today find their greatest difficulty. They can
believe in a spiritual Being, an Eternal Spirit, who is

the Father of the spirits of men, but they cannot believe that a God of love is supreme in the outward course of the world and of their individual lives. So many things happen which, if we attribute them to the hand of God, would seem to make of him a monster of unreasoning cruelty. When we cease to believe in a God who is almighty, belief in a blind fate is all that is left for us. In the face of that, the best we can do is, with the heroism of the humanist, to cherish a courageous despair. What is at stake here is the unity of the whole of life. The question is whether or not it is true that all things have meaning and purpose in relation to God and, therefore, in relation to our lives. In the bitter experience of today and the happy experience of tomorrow, can I believe that my life is in the hands of God and that he is using these things to work out his purpose with me? That is the faith we must have if we are to face all our tomorrows with courage and with hope — a faith that God is on the throne and that everything that comes to us he uses somehow to effect his own glory and our blessedness. It is not by chance that wherever in the Bible a triumphant faith comes to expression it is always a faith in a sovereign God. There can be no triumph for our faith, no real jubilation, no overcoming of the world, unless our God is also Lord.

The usual objection to the sovereignty of God is that it makes of God an Oriental monarch instead of a loving Father. The objection has its justification in the tendency of an older theology to picture God too often as a tyrant to be feared, rather than a father to be loved. But, in the swing of the pendulum away from that old inadequate idea of God, the truth of the real sovereignty of God has been allowed to pass out of sight and out of mind. The God of love has become a mildly sentimental Being beyond the skies who stands in no definite relationship to the actualities of life. All the iron backbone of reality has gone out of faith.

That we believe in a God who is Sovereign and Lord means that we accept our life situation each day, whatever it may be, as the creation, not of a blind fate, but of a God of justice, truth, and love. Like Jesus in Gethsemane, we can take the heaviest cross and, even in the moment of sharpest agony and darkness, because of what God is we can be sure that there is a purpose and a meaning in it all. We do not waste our time and spiritual energy, then, knocking our heads vainly against the imperfections of our circumstances. Where we are is the starting point God has given us, and all we ask is where his will is to lead us from there. That is the faith which overcomes the world. Because our God is Lord of all the days, we face into the future with an assurance that the unfolding of the days and years must in the very nature of things be an unfolding ever more fully of God's plans and God's purposes for us.

It is in relation to this that the old doctrine of predestination is to be understood. No doctrine has been more distorted by both its proponents and its opponents. To most persons it suggests pure fatalism, a belief that what is to be will be. However, we can safely defy any-one to find fatalism in the Biblical conception of a sover-eign God. Its whole effect, as we see it in the prophets, in the psalmists, and in New Testament believers, is the very opposite to that of fatalism. There is in it nothing of a passive acceptance of life's evils, but the most vigor-ous and active combating of them. There is this in it: The events of our lives are never the futile blunderings of chance: there is always a divine purpose hidden in them. The events themselves may be the result of our own folly or of someone else's actions: a mother neglects her health and falls a prey to disease; a car driver strikes and kills a young child. We cannot interpret such things as though God sat in heaven and said: " Let that mother die. Let that child be struck." Predestination so interpreted would make of God a horrible being. But it *does* mean that nothing can happen to us which will be outside God's purpose for us. Whatever our situation may be, God's will for us runs like a thread through those concrete circumstances, and by faith we can dis-cover it, embrace it, and rejoice in it. God has a purpose for each of us, and he shows his sovereignty in being able to make everything that happens to us serve that purpose and be comprehended in it.

Sometimes men profess to find a contrast between the

Old Testament Sovereign God and the New Testament Father God. The contrast is misplaced, for in the Old Testament God's mercy and love are fundamental, and in the New Testament there is no thought of God the Father except as the Almighty, the Sovereign. It is noteworthy that Jesus more than once in his parables likened God's relationship to man to that of a landowner to his steward. It was a familiar likeness in the ancient world. Potiphar entrusted Joseph with the management of his great Egyptian estates. Joseph was as free in the administration of them as any man could wish to be free. But always he knew that what passed through his hands was not his own, and that one day he would have to give an accounting of his stewardship. Thus Jesus in his parables is insisting that the ownership of all things is God's, and that man is never owner, but only steward. What he has — his life, his talents, his possessions — belongs to God and it is given to him for his lifetime as a sacred trust.

Again and again throughout the Scriptures this claim of God upon the whole of life is enunciated. The psalmist says, " The earth is the Lord's and the fulness thereof; the world, and they that dwell therein." The prophet is herald of a God whose commands cannot be isolated in a " religious " sphere, but have to do with every aspect of life. Therefore the basic sin of life is that man acts as though he were not steward but owner, as though he had no Master over him to whom he is accountable. He asserts a freedom, which he even presumes at times to call a God-given freedom, to do as he likes with what is his own. There is much of this in the pervasive individualism of our day. Intrinsically, it is an assertion of our right of ownership against God's right of ownership. It is a repudiation of the claim that God makes upon our lives in every part of his Word. In fact, this is the denial of God, the atheism of action, which flourishes often in the midst of piety and professing Christianity. As such, it is far more sinister than all the theoretical atheism about which Christians become so disturbed. Only a dishonest man will find the examples of it exclusively in other men.

There is no believing in God without acceptance of God's sovereignty, and there is no acceptance of his sovereignty without that humbling of the human self in which man finds his rightful place as a steward of God. But when a man begins to live with this Master over him and to deal with everything in his life, not as owner, but as steward, he finds that " under God's sovereignty " and " in God's Kingdom " mean one and the same thing. And he learns also what Jesus meant when he said, " Henceforth I call you not servants; . . . but friends."

Chapter 5

Jesus Christ, His Son

Our God Is Not a Creature of Our Imaginations

AN ACCUSATION against religion which we hear from time to time is that its gods are purely imaginary beings; they are projections into the outer world of our inner thoughts and desires, and, therefore, have reality only in our own minds. Primitive men took wood or clay or gold or silver and shaped with it a god before which to bow down and worship. We are more refined. We shape a god for ourselves out of ideas. Then by an effort of imagination we set that god on a throne in the heavens and bow ourselves down in worship. The one procedure is as foolish and self-deluded as the other, say our accusers. The sharp point of their criticism, which does disturb us, is that to a great degree it is true. Far too often the God we worship and the Christ we worship are mere creations of our own imaginations, without one breath of reality in them. When that is true, our worship and belief become hollow and unreal, a stagnant pool within ourselves.

How often in prayer there is a haunting consciousness that the God to whom we are praying has no
reality but that which our minds give to him! In our
praying we do not get outside of ourselves; it remains
a sterile process from which we come away secretly
ashamed. From what we have been told, and have read,
and have imagined for ourselves, we have shaped our
conception of God. Conceive him as perfectly as we
may, we know full well that not yet have we found him
as a Living God. God himself has not come over the
horizon of our life so that in our prayer we can with
full meaning say " I " and " Thou." In the Bible, however, God is never an abstract Being concerning whom
men have ideas, but a definite Person who with definiteness makes himself known to man. The God of the Bible
is always a God who is dealing with men and with nations in the concrete events and experiences of life. Our
minds are not left to sweep through uninhabited spaces
seeking where we may find him. He is the One who has
ordered the past, who orders the present, and who will,
in days to come, order all that makes up our life. He is
before us, and behind us, and round about us on every
side, so that we cannot escape from him. We are in his
hand. Reconciliation with him is thus not a transaction
with a spiritual Being somewhere distant in the heavens;
nor is it a mystic experience of the " inner " life. It is
reconciliation with Him who has made our life such as

it is. There is no meaning in it except as it enables us
to find his good and perfect will in the place he has given
us and the tasks he has set for us in life.

One of the prime characteristics of our Christian belief in God is just this realism. The mystic religious imagination is given no scope. If we are to find God, we
must find him in the actualities of our life, past, present,
and future. We may speculate about God to our heart's
delight, but it is with the God who orders our life that
we must make our peace. That God, we know well, is
no mere projection of our own minds, for in him we
meet again and again a will that is not our will, and
ways which most certainly are not the ways that we
would choose.

Turning now to the subject of belief in Christ, the
same distinction is required between the imaginary and
the real. The Christ whom many worship is almost entirely an imaginary being. They think of him very much
as they do of God — as a rather vague and remote
heavenly Person. A kindly pleasant soul, the perfection
of all ideals, dwelling far off in the ethereal regions, he
might be called either God or Christ without its making much difference. Very likely, the effect of such belief
upon life is not one whit other than the effect upon life
of the belief of an ancient Greek in one of the nobler of
his gods — a strengthening of the hold of ideals upon
life through objectifying them, and the feeling of assur-

ance lent by the thought of a favorable overruling Spirit. This imaginary Christ is, not the Master, but rather the slave of man. His image is shaped imperceptibly to fit most comfortably man's own desires, to the end that he may believe in his Christ with the least effort and difficulty possible.

Our Christian faith, however, leaves us no room for such fatal exercise of the imagination. The Christ in whom we believe is a definite Person, of whose life and spirit and sayings a record has been preserved for us. He is what he is, and says what he says, regardless of what we think or desire. We can take offense at him and turn away from him; we can praise him or condemn him as we please. But change him we cannot; nor can we make him other than what he is.

The powerlessness of much of our Christianity and the deadness we so often find in our personal faith have their source in this substitution of a man-made Christ for the God-made one. Our Christ has become a colorless figure, repeating platitudes unceasingly, instead of the actual Person who meets us in the Gospels, whose words are like sharp daggers. That process of devitalizing goes on constantly in all of us, and we are bound to be falling away to a false Christ unless we come back again and again to the Gospels and let the true Christ be lifted up before our eyes. It is so convenient to forget that Jesus says, " Love your enemies." It is so com-

forting to think that Jesus would not expect more of
us than that we should live a decent life. If we keep
away from the Gospels, it is surprising how quickly we
can have him saying only the things that are pleasant
for us to hear. But when we open our Bibles, at once it
is another voice we hear, a Voice which commands, a
Voice which searches out weaknesses in us that we had
not dreamed were there, a Voice which speaks the plain
truth to us regardless of how unpleasant or offensive it
may be. Equally unexpected are the promises that the
Voice utters. With this Voice we must reckon and in
this Person must we believe if we are to have a Christian
faith. Here again we see how concrete are the bases of
our Christian belief in God. Just as God the Father Almighty is God meeting us in the actualities of our daily
life, so Christ, the Son of God, is God meeting us in a
human life, in a historical person, whose words and actions and purposes and principles can be placed before
us with clearness for decision.

The Human Story

Who is this Jesus whom men call the Christ, the Son
of God? That is the question with which we are confronted. The first answer that comes to us is that he was
a man, a human being like ourselves, born into this world
on a certain day long ago, looking no different from any

of a hundred million other babies. A short life was his, little more than thirty years, and lived in an obscure corner of the earth, the tiny land of Palestine, which is not much larger than a pair of our counties. Yet even in that small sphere he cannot be said to have attained in his lifetime to any measure of prominence. For nearly thirty years he did nothing publicly of any particular note. He grew up in Nazareth, playing in the streets as any boy plays, roaming over the hills and fields, and going to school. The eldest of a large family (there seem to have been at least seven children in the home), he had the responsibility of filling the place of the father, both in the carpenter shop and in the home, from the time of his father's death. If you were able to jump back over the centuries and ask some of the good folk of Nazareth your question, " Who is this Jesus? " they would answer, " He is that young fellow down the street who takes such good care of his family and makes a fine job of our plows and implements when we take them to him to have them repaired." They might re- mark upon some peculiarities that set him aside from the ordinary run of men, but that would be all.

When he was thirty years old, to the surprise and as- tonishment of his family and his townsmen, he gave up his carpentering (perhaps a younger brother took over the shop and the care of the family), and began a mis- sion of teaching and healing. His message was in many

ways like that of the great prophets of Israel. In fact,
he deliberately linked himself up with them. He took
something of their method and he found himself standing directly in line with their teaching. With John the
Baptist, who was a typical Old Testament prophet, he
had close fellowship. But these were only starting points
from which he went on to work out his own unique message to men and to fulfill his own unique ministry. He
soon attained a considerable degree of respect and recognition as a religious teacher. Some orthodox rabbis,
who as a rule paid no heed to anyone not educated in
the regular rabbinical schools, held his abilities in high
esteem. With the common people he was extremely
popular for a time. This was due partly to their response
to his devotion to them, but largely to their misconcep-
tion of his purpose, their idea that soon he would bring
the world order, and with it the Roman domination, to
an end, and would usher in the Messianic Age. When he
disillusioned them and forced them to see the real nature
of his Gospel, his popularity dwindled and faded away.

As it became increasingly clear that the teachings of
Jesus would necessarily result in a new kind of religion,
and that this would spell disaster for the old faith of
the fathers, he met with bitter opposition and the forces
took shape which were eventually to carry him to his
death. Some of the disciples whom he had gathered
round him shrank from the conflict and would gladly

have evaded it. Jesus himself seems never to have wavered. Calmly he went on with his teaching and his healing until the storm of opposition overtook him. As the shadow of the cross fell directly across his way, he had his hour of bitter struggle in Gethsemane. But from then to the end, with the same calm mastery as before, he went straight on as one who was finishing the work it was given him to do. Soon all that was left was a poor breathless body hanging upon a cross outside the city walls.

That is the story in brief. Some Christians refuse to see the full humanity of that life, and thereby they blind themselves to much of its meaning. They begin by attributing to Jesus such divine qualities as omniscience — that he knew all things at all times — and omnipotence — that he was really all-powerful and his weakness only a seeming weakness. They think that they are maintaining the divinity of Jesus when all they are doing is robbing him of the full humanity which God gave to him and at the same time confusing the meaning of his divinity. Jesus was man. Give to the words in Luke 2:52 their full significance, that Jesus as a boy had to *grow,* not only in body, but in mind and spirit. Take it as literal truth that he was tempted in all points like as we are. He felt the sharpness of the same temptations that touch us, and he had to conquer them and put them under his feet. He was flesh of our flesh. He laughed and cried. He was lifted up and he was cast down. He entered into our common human experiences. That is, in human terms, a little of the answer we have to give to the question, Who is this Jesus?

The Deeper Claim

Now, of this one man of all the millions of men who have ever lived, of this one teacher of all the religious teachers the world has known, the astounding claim is made that God himself was incarnate in him. He was the Son of God, the Saviour of the world. Many Christians take that claim for granted so easily and unthinkingly that they do not see how stupendous it is. It is no wonder that men have mocked at it and have drawn back from it, for it is, looked at from the outside, an essentially unbelievable thing — that this young Jew who died before he was thirty-three should be the incarnation of God himself.

The claim is made from three different quarters. Jesus himself was convinced that he was the Saviour of the world and that in him was being opened up a new and perfect way for God to come to men and men to 'God. It is not only when he speaks of his Messiahship and in his assertions such as, " I am the light of the world," and, " I am the way, the truth, and the life," that this is evident. Constantly in his teaching, the under-

lying assumption is that he, Jesus, stands at the center
of all life. This is plainly to be seen in an appeal such
as, " Come unto me, all ye that labour and are heavy
laden, and I will give you rest." When we compare those
words with the appeals and promises made by the prophets and psalmists, we see that Jesus is consciously plac-
ing himself where God has always stood; he is promising to men what from of old they have hoped to find
only in God. Those who think that they can separate
Jesus' ethical and religious teachings from the claims of
Messiahship that are made for his person are doomed
to disappointment. Take away every vestige of his conviction of centrality and Messiahship, and what is left
is like a tent from which the center pole has been removed. Our estimation of Jesus cannot leave this claim
out of account. If Jesus was mistaken in it, we have no
alternative but to adjudge him an insanely egotistical
religious teacher. But when we look at his life and teaching we find no trace of what we know to be the invariable
accompaniments of such egotism. When he sets himself
at the center, it is because there has come to him the
humbling recognition that in the eternal order of things
he *belongs* at the center.

The claim was made a second time by those who came
under Jesus' influence during the years of his ministry,
but never as a mere repetition of Jesus' own words. They

knew him as a man among men, but as his influence upon their lives deepened, they found themselves in relation to him confronted with decisions that were a choice between God and self. In order to remain in fellowship with him, they had to let themselves be transformed and lifted into a new life. When they tried to put in words what had happened to them through him, they had to say that it was God who had sought them and found them in him. Out of the depths of his heart and life Peter confessed, " Thou art the Christ, the Son of the living God."

We need not confine ourselves to the immediate disciples. Let us ask our question, " Who is this Jesus? " of the woman who crept like a beggar into Simon's house when Jesus was at supper there, and went away with a soul as pure as a child's and with peace flooding all her being. Let us ask her who Jesus was and see what answer she has to give us. Or let us ask Zacchaeus what it was he saw in Jesus' eyes that day in Jericho that made him change his whole course of life from that time on. They would tell us simply that in Jesus they met face to face the Saviour of man. God was in Christ, reconciling them unto himself.

But that is not all. The claim is made a third time by people who never once saw Jesus in the flesh. Paul is our best New Testament example. His witness has force

added to it by the fact that he started from a settled
and well-rooted conviction of the falsity of the claim.
To Paul, and to all orthodox Jews, it was both absurd
and blasphemous for Jesus to put himself in the place
which, they knew, belonged to God alone. When Jesus
forgave men their sins, the rabbis were sharp to notice that he was exercising one of the prerogatives of
God. The authority with which he taught was also a
source of provocation. He seemed to speak with finality,
as though his pronouncement were the last word, super-
seding all that came before. It was with relief that they
saw him nailed to his cross, for they had not been without plaguing doubts. The thought must have come to
them in quiet moments that perhaps they themselves
were wrong. His crucifixion, however, seemed to give
objective proof that Jesus was only a man and not the
Son of God.

For some the matter was not yet settled. In the mind
of Paul, the truth of what Jesus was in himself remained
as a sharp goad to torment him. Down underneath there
was an unacknowledged recognition that what Jesus had
brought to men was what he, Paul, had long been seeking for himself. Even while Paul was proving to his
mind that Jesus was not the Christ, that in Jesus which
made Him the Christ was forcing Paul into a corner and
compelling the reluctant submission of his heart and life.
Finally, on the Damascus road the struggle came to an

end, and Paul from that time forth was ready to give
to Jesus a name that was above every name.

That is the beginning of the testimony, and it con-
tinues like a stream down through the centuries, sometimes wide and deep, sometimes narrow and shallow.
We do not need to pay attention to those who call Jesus
the Saviour and the Son of God merely because they
have read it or have heard it from someone else. There
are others who, if we find them, can tell us whom they
have met with in Jesus of Nazareth, how he has transformed life for them, and how he pours in upon them in
abundance the riches of the spirit. He does for us what
only God can do. He says to us what only God can say.
He gives us what only God can give. What else, then,
can we say than that God is in him reconciling us unto
himself?

Perhaps someone will say, " But you have not proved
to us that Jesus is the Christ, the Son of God, nor have
you shown us how we can believe in him." The writer
of the Gospel of John, when he wanted to bring men to
a belief in Christ, did not give any proof; nor had he
anything to say about the " how " of faith. He lifted up
Jesus before men's eyes, showed him as he himself had
found him, as the Saviour and Lord and Light of life.
He left the matter there, confident that if men would
look with open eyes, or perhaps we should say with
opened eyes, they would see and believe. We cannot

prove to anyone that Jesus is the Christ. We cannot *show* a man how to believe. What we *can* do, by preaching Christ and teaching Christ, by letting his spirit so master us that it will shine out through our words and actions, is to glorify him and witness to him before men, so that today through us he will still exercise his ministry, bringing men under judgment by his holiness and opening to them the way of salvation by his love.

It may seem strange that this chapter on our belief in Jesus Christ is the shortest of all, when we should expect it to be given the most attention. There is a reason for the shortness. To go farther would involve entering into a detailed discussion of his life and teachings and of his person. It would lead us into questions with which we cannot begin to deal here. It is sufficient for our present purpose to have suggested what it means to call Jesus the Christ.

However, let it not be thought that he can be known as the Christ apart from his life and teachings. Any belief in him that is not a response of our whole beings — heart, mind and will — to the living reality which confronts us in every segment of his teachings and his life, is a false and hollow belief. Belief in him is not evoked by talking about his Christhood, but by retelling the old, old story of his words and his works. That brings us to the agelong task of the Church, a task that will never be done as long as the world stands: to be a human body through which Jesus may speak his words and work his works in the world of today. Only as men are brought face to face with the reality of Jesus Christ in Christian people does there come to them any comprehension of what is meant by the words " Jesus Christ " in the Gospels.

Chapter 6

Christ Crucified

CHRISTIANS have been called morbid because they insist on calling to mind again and again a ghastly death. Men say: "Why must you talk about Jesus' death? His life and his teachings are so much more interesting and agreeable and profitable as a subject." Our answer is that the Jesus of whom we talk is not Jesus the Christ unless we see him and hear him and think of him always as the crucified One.

Jesus' disciples had many intimate hours with him. They thought they knew him. Yet their testimony is that the fullness of the meaning of his life did not break in upon them until he had died for them. For Paul the death of Jesus was the key which alone unlocked the secret of all his life and teaching. The death is incomprehensible apart from the life, and the life is incomprehensible apart from the death.

When a man is painting a picture his full plan may remain hidden until the last stroke of the brush. All his strokes keep giving us suggestions of his meaning, but in its fullness it does not stand revealed until he is done.

That last touch gives a new significance to every detail of the picture. So is it with the cross. We do not understand Jesus, nor do we understand aright any part of our faith, until we see all in the light of the cross. The Church is not just a gathering together of people interested in religion and morality. It is a Church under the cross. We call ourselves followers of the Christ, but it changes the whole content of those words when we are reminded that the Christ we follow is Christ crucified.

One of the deficiencies of many of our Protestant Churches is that we have nowhere in evidence, either within or without, the symbol of the cross. In fact, if we were to place crosses on our Church steeples, or if we were to hang great crosses in the front of our Churches, that the cross might be before the eyes of all in worship, there would most likely be a vehement reaction. People would be horrified, and we should hear them asking whether we were trying to make our Church into a Roman Catholic Church. But to whom does the symbol of the cross belong? What Church has any prior claim upon it? We have said that the cross is at the center of all true faith, and that our Church is a Church under the cross. If that is true, is it not strange that in many of our Churches the sign of the cross is nowhere to be seen? If we let it vanish in like manner from our thoughts, from our faith, and from our lives, we shall have ceased to be worthy to bear the name " Christian."

The Fact of the Cross

The cross must first be seen as a historic fact. There are many today who say that what they want in their religion is facts, solid facts. Let them take the fact of the cross and see what they can make of it. Let them omit nothing, neither the high moral and religious standing of those who sent Jesus to his death nor the awful details of the death itself — the nails driven through the hands and feet and the sensitive body left hanging there in agony until life was extinct. What does it mean that he who came " to preach the gospel to the poor, . . . to heal the broken-hearted, to preach deliverance to the captives, and recovering of sight to the blind " should in *our* world have had to die such a death?

First, we must see what the forces were which led to Jesus' execution. It was not the achievement of malicious and perverse Jews, as many seem to think. He was put to death because his work threatened the future of existing institutions. Early in Jesus' ministry there were leaders among the Jews who perceived the danger of his teaching. The faith of the fathers would soon crumble into ruins if the people began to pay too serious heed to the revolutionary teachings of this Galilean prophet. Jesus was making no secret of the fact that the religion he taught could get along quite well without any of the paraphernalia of the established religion. It could dispense even with the Temple. At every turn Jesus' teachings were an affront to the rabbis and were undermining the authority of the old religion. In the face of this danger, patriotism and loyalty to the old faith demanded militant action. The fire had to be stamped out before it could spread and cause a general conflagration. Thus, it was the loyalty of conscientious men to their religion which, more than anything else, caused Jesus' death.

Financial considerations may also have played a part. Jerusalem businessmen depended then as now upon the religious pilgrims for their trade. Let that great stream of pilgrim traffic dry up and the financial loss to Jerusalem would be reckoned in millions. It was known that Jesus was telling men they could worship God as effectually in any part of the earth as in Jerusalem. If men were to take that seriously, the commercial life of Jerusalem would be ruined.

Then there were the Romans, with their anxiety to preserve order. What was the death of one more Galilean if it might nip in the bud a new uprising against the Roman authority?

These and other factors are part of the description of Jesus' death, and need to be kept in mind if the cross is to be truly a revelation of life for us. We cannot divorce the cross from its setting or we lose touch with its meaning. We look at what actually happened and then begin to ask: Why had there to be a cross? What difference does it make to me that there was a cross?

The Necessity of the Cross

The cross, first of all, witnesses to the integrity of Jesus. It tells us of the completeness with which he was committed to his own Gospel. Men always expect a certain disparity between teaching and doing, for they themselves would not want to be held to the full discharge of their doctrine. Thus Peter thought that his words were only common sense when he advised Jesus to put out of his mind the burdensome prospect of a violent death. Peter could not see the direct and necessary road that led from Jesus' teaching to the cross. He knew that the teaching and the claims of Jesus, maintained at their full value, must lead to an impasse with the authorities. A diplomatic softening of the tone of both, just enough to avoid the issue, did not seem to him to be out of the question.

The Church and individual Christians, through the years, have known only too well how to engineer such diplomatic softening of the tones of the Gospel and of the claims of Christ when the tension between God's truth and the world has reached the danger point. In a time of unusual tension like our own it is perhaps inevitable that these gifts of diplomacy should be highly prized in many sections of the Church and that straight-forward speaking of the truth only too often should be deprecated as " extremist." Nothing takes away more quickly the discomfort which the Word of God creates in the soul of a man than to discover that the man through whom the Word has come does not himself take it with complete seriousness. The escape from that discomfort is an escape from God and from our own salvation.

Jesus by his cross blocked effectually any such way of escape. No man can find any point at which he turned aside from the truth with which he had been confronting and affronting men. His word and his deed are one. They would not have remained one, however, had he evaded the cross. That fatal disparity between teaching and doing would have crept in. By it the integrity of Jesus which gives him such an overwhelming appeal to the heart and mind of man would have been destroyed.

There is perhaps a clue here to the reason why " our " Gospel and " our " Christianity fails often to make any impression upon the minds of thoughtful men. The world knows what we ought to know but evidently have forgotten — that when a man really believes in any-thing he lets his whole fate become bound up with it. That is the only kind of belief that even men of the world can respect. What are they to think, then, when they see Christians who are not even embarrassed by the radical differences between the principles of the Gospel which they profess and teach and the principles which actuate their conduct in everyday life?

The Gospel says, " Forgive your enemies; forgive seventy times seven." This or that Churchman says, " I guess I am not a good enough Christian yet for that." The man of the world says, " Why not be honest and admit you do not believe in it? " It is not too much to say that men are actually *prevented* from believing by this lack of integrity in professing Christians. They cannot be expected to take the Christian faith seriously as long as they see Christians acting as though they were not much in earnest about it.

When Christians begin to learn the meaning of loyalty and integrity at the cross, when they become, not just embarrassed, but in the deepest sense humiliated, by the gulf between their profession and their performance, then again today God will be using the cross to disturb and to redeem the world.

If we are to understand, however, why Jesus said to his disciples that he *must* be killed, we shall have to look farther than the necessity within himself that his truth and his life should remain one. At the very beginning of his ministry he was convinced that a tragic death was involved in his destiny as the Messiah. There can be no doubt that Jesus pondered long over his Old Testament as he sought to understand the full meaning of his Messiahship and that he found a definite foreshadowing there of what was to be involved in his own mission. That lesser entrance of God's Word into history which took place in the prophets made plain the inevitable pattern of events when the world should find itself confronted with God's truth incarnate.

The words heard by Jesus at his baptism take us back into his understanding of the Old Testament in respect to himself. There is a twofold Messianic significance in what he heard. " This is my beloved Son " comes from the Second Psalm, and " in whom I am well pleased " from the forty-second chapter of Isaiah. Their coming together in the mind of Jesus indicates that he saw in himself the fulfillment of Israel's agelong expectation of the Messiah and also of the prophetic Servant of God so vividly pictured in the latter half of the book of Isaiah. Again, when he wished to make known to his fellow townsmen in Nazareth the nature of the mission on which he was embarking, he read to them in the synagogue a passage from these same pages of Isaiah in which the Servant of God describes his office.

But if Jesus related such passages directly to himself, what must have been his thoughts when chapters fifty and fifty-three of Isaiah lay open before him? He could not take to himself " In whom I am well pleased " and " The Spirit of the Lord God is upon me " without also

taking to himself " I gave my back to the smiters " and
" He was numbered with the transgressors; and he bare
the sin of many." He read, " Surely he hath borne our
griefs, and carried our sorrows " and knew that this was
what he had come into the world to do. Then he read on:
" He was wounded for our transgressions. . . . It
pleased the Lord to bruise him." One thinks of the long
hours when Jesus turned over and over in his mind the
significance of these words for the days that lay before
him. From the very beginning he had seen right to the
end of his road and had counted all the cost. The taking
up of his Messiahship was the taking up of his cross.

That such thoughts as these were in Jesus' mind at
the time of his baptism appears all the more likely if
we press the question, Why did Jesus undergo John's
baptism? It was a baptism of repentance for the remis-
sion of sins. What sins had Jesus to repent of? What
cleansing did *he* need? None, we say. Why, then, did he
insist upon being baptized and override John's objections and reluctance?

It was not for his own sake that he did this, but for
the sake of others. " For their sakes I sanctify myself,"
he said on another occasion. He was numbering himself
with the transgressors, although he was no transgressor, identifying himself with men in their unrighteous-
ness, and taking the burden of their sins upon him as
though it were his own. A mother or father whose child

has fallen into some shameful sin can understand what he was doing. They too, because of their love for the child, enter into the guilt of another life than their own. It is not their sin, yet they feel the shame and the burden of it as though it were their own.

Thus in himself, in a soul unstained, Jesus felt the guilt and the uncleanness and the weight of condemnation which everywhere is pressing down upon men because of their sin. He felt it as no man has ever felt it. Already in his baptism he was at his work of bearing men's sins in the sense of taking them upon himself and bearing them away. It was as though he were putting his shoulders under the whole monstrous load of human sin which had so long been corrupting and perverting and overwhelming the heart of man, that he might in himself carry it off and dump it into the depths of the sea. Having begun the task of sin-bearing, could he have failed to see that before he was through with it it would cost him his life? The evidence is that he not only saw it clearly, but that he tried, and tried in vain, to make his disciples understand what must be the final issue of his Messiahship.

Why did the destiny of the Messiah, the work of the Sin Bearer, involve suffering and death? Because that very necessity is written deeply into the nature of the world and the nature of the God to whom the world belongs. We have become so superficial in our understand-

ing of evil, thinking of it merely as error, that enlightenment seems sufficient to deliver mankind from all evil
and to transform the world into the Kingdom of God.
Yet one of the basic insights of the Scriptures has to do
with the nature of evil. It is not just absence of light,
but an insidious, aggressive power at work everywhere
in life, cunningly deceiving men and seeking in the most
unexpected ways to draw them away from allegiance to
God into the entanglements of an evil bondage. It can
and does use even what seems to be praiseworthy religiousness and morality as a defense against God, behind which a part of life may be kept free from the
claims of God. Thus the strength of evil is that it appears, not as evil, but in forms that men recognize as
good. Evil that is plainly evil has little power. But when
evil has dressed itself in the garments of righteousness
and piety, it has colossal power. This explains why Jesus
had little to say about drunkenness and kindred sins, but
much to say about hypocrisy and self-righteousness.
The reversal of emphasis in the present-day Church
arises from the loss of the Biblical insight into the nature of evil.

Today we cannot conceive of a cultured, respectable
man being actually an evil man and an enemy of God,
for we have unconsciously had our standards of judgment formed from other quarters than the Scriptures.
There is a direct line which leads from this loss of in-

sight into the nature of evil in our modern world to the unrestrained and staggering upthrust of evil forces that our modern society has experienced. We are perhaps ready today to listen when the Scriptures tell us that evil is more, much more, than error. But are we ready to hear that the natural condition of man, in spite of all the culture and morality and religious sentiments that he may possess, is one of alienation from God; that even when he is telling himself that he is seeking God and trying to live the good life, forces are at work in him that set him in antagonism to the will of God? The stronghold of those forces is the stubborn determination of the self within him to remain master and sovereign within its own realm. It will make concessions, even great concessions, to God as long as it is not forced to capitulate. When that last issue is pressed, strange things may happen, for evil is being threatened in its deepest and strongest lair.

Man's Judgment and God's Triumph

If the Messiah was to deliver man from his sin, he had to unmask it, to challenge it, and to overcome it in its stronghold. This Jesus believed that he was doing by his death, and the testimony of his first disciples and of his Church through the centuries has been that his death has nothing less than this cosmic significance. As Jesus

himself expressed it, as recorded in John 12:31, his
death was the judgment of the world, and the expulsion
of the Prince of Evil.

We are accustomed to think of the judgment of the
world only in terms of an event that is to occur at the
end of time or a solemn ordeal that awaits the soul at
death. Jesus, however, spoke of it in the present tense,
and the plain meaning of his words is that it was to be
achieved by his death. If we think in legal terms of ju-
dicial processes, with passing of sentence and punishment, we shall miss the true significance. We ought to
think rather of the use of the word " judgment " by the
Old Testament prophets, where God's judgment upon
Israel was seen in definite historical events. The approach of an enemy or the coming of famine was interpreted as a judgment upon the nation's sin. It was not
by any means purely a matter of punishment; it was
judgment in the sense of laying bare the horror of sin
with its consequences. The word " judgment " might
thus be defined as a disastrous event which makes evident and brings into the full light the evil that has been
lying hidden. We can speak of judgments of this kind
in the case of individuals. A businessman may gradually
get into the habit of little dishonesties, considering them
justified on the ground of common practice. But one day
they involve him in ruin; he wakens from his self-decep-
tion to find himself disgraced. His misfortune is a judg-

ment of God, an event which brings to light suddenly the hidden, unrecognized evil.

Jesus, in saying that his cross is the judgment of the whole world, meant that it is the event which brings out into the open the hidden, life-poisoning evil of the world, and reveals God's mind, God's judgment, concerning us. If we were asked *our* judgment concerning the world, we would answer that it is a place where there are some good people and some bad people, and a mass of people who belong somewhere in between. We see men in an infinitely long gradation between good and evil, some quite high in the scale, and some quite low. We try to comfort ourselves by feeling that we are reasonably high up in the scale as compared with other men, and we try to be humble by leaving a long space between our position and the top of the scale. That is the way *we* judge the world. When we ask *God's* judgment concerning the world, however, the answer is more abrupt. He says, " The world crucified the Lord of glory." But, we say to ourselves, that cannot possibly mean us, for see how high we are in the scale of goodness! We forget that the Jews and Romans who sent Jesus to death were also quite high up in the scale of goodness. They were not rogues or villains, but the best-living and the most cultured men of their day. Yet they crucified the Lord of glory. Judas was a Christian preacher and missionary.

Behind all our goodness and our virtue, our wisdom, our culture, and our religion, there may lurk something unknown to us that can make us enemies of God. We are no more secure than were those Jews. We have no better reason for confidence that we are on the side of God than they had. The cross is God's judgment upon us all, which makes us see what it is in the heart of the world and in our hearts to do. It destroys our self-security and self-confidence and leaves us in complete uncertainty. That is what God meant it to do. Our spiritual security and pride and self-righteousness are the roots of evil in life. Yet they pass as angels of light until the cross reveals them to us as the powers of the Prince of Darkness.

The cross, however, is not merely a revelation of the nature of our sin, showing us that we are all without excuse before God and, therefore, without basis for setting ourselves up above our brothers. It is also the one decisive conquest of the power of evil. " Now shall the prince of this world be cast out." The only power that evil has comes from deception. It has to pass itself off as something good and justifiable. If it is brought out into the light and seen *as it is,* it loses its power. It must work always in darkness, with its real nature hidden. The world sees the struggle between good and evil as a struggle between good and bad men. The attention of men in general is concentrated upon the transformation

or elimination of these bad men in order to bring a new
day for the world. The cross says to us that the real
stronghold of evil may not be in bad men at all. Evil
may have its most powerful agents in good, religious,
conscientious men who think that they are on the side of
God. Their goodness, and religiousness, and conscien-
tiousness give evil its prestige and enable it to accom-
plish just such acts as the Crucifixion of Jesus Christ.

Let men who adopt the attitude that man needs a religion and that any of the higher religions is adequate
for him, take account of this: *Religion* crucified Jesus
Christ. To me, that says that my religion and my goodness are not enough. It wakens me to the fact that I
may at this moment be unconsciously serving the Prince
of this world, and not God. When that awakening comes
and all human security is broken down, I am ready to be
led step by step by the hand of God. I know what a des-
perately earnest and perilous thing it is that I am a sinner. I know that I must be led each step of the way by
his grace and guidance if I am not to go astray. When
human pride and self-sufficiency are so broken that man
is willing to live humbly by the daily bread of God's
grace, the Prince of this world is cast out.

" And I, if I be lifted up . . . will draw all men unto
me." There is a strange drawing power in the cross. Before we have thought much about it we have felt it, the
cross exerting a power upon us like a magnet upon the

steel. The cross draws us out of ourselves and up to God because it judges us and sets us where we belong in life. Because it breaks the power of evil over us by humbling our pride, the cross and the cross alone has the power to deliver us from the imprisonment and darkness of our self-will, and to bring us into our true heritage as the sons of God. A Jesus who merely enlightens us where we are in error leaves us still in bondage. A Christ who, in the boundlessness of his love for us, suffers and dies for our sakes smites us to the heart, slays self in us, and, taking from us all lesser freedoms, selfish freedoms, makes us sharers of the freedom of the spirit which is his own.

Chapter 7

The Holy Spirit

THERE IS an incident recorded in Scripture which confronts us with the phenomenon of a group of people who consider themselves Christians but know nothing of the Holy Spirit. Paul said unto them: " Have ye received the Holy Spirit since ye believed? And they said unto him, We have not so much as heard whether there be any Holy Spirit." Acts 19:2. No better starting point for consideration of the subject of the Holy Spirit could be found than this passage. As for the phenomenon itself, were the truth told, it is rather the rule than the exception among Christians today.

We can only surmise the nature of the Christianity that the people of Ephesus learned from Apollos, the Alexandrian missionary. They would know something of Jesus' teachings and of the story of his life and death. A man with an Alexandrian background would be likely to present the Gospel to them as a philosophy of life. This they had accepted and were trying to put into practice. But when Paul asked them whether they had received the Holy Spirit, they were at a loss to understand

147

him. This was a spiritual power with which they were wholly unacquainted.

Christianity Without the Holy Spirit

Our present situation is camouflaged by our familiarity with the words " Holy Spirit." The words are repeated so often in our hearing, we take them so much upon our own lips, that we almost persuade ourselves we know the reality of them, when actually we know only the words. The truth is that the type of Christianity commonest in the Churches is identical with that of the Ephesian disciples before the coming of Paul.

Let us describe this type of Christian more definitely. He has heard in the Gospel the challenge to a higher life and has responded to it in his own way. He has set himself what he regards as a Christian standard of living and would be ashamed to fall below that standard. He looks trustingly to God as his Heavenly Father and with some warmth of affection would call Jesus Christ his Saviour. He has a Christian philosophy of life. Nevertheless, were Paul to put to him the pointed question which he asked these Ephesian folk, " Have ye received the Holy Spirit since ye believed? " he would in honesty be forced to answer " No." There is no reality, no spiritual presence, in his life which corresponds with these words " Holy Spirit."

Some may be inclined to defend the type of Christian which has been described. They would not expect any man's Christianity to go farther than his. They would be well content were the religion of all men to reach that standard, and they cannot see that the omission of the Holy Spirit results in any essential loss. In fact, it may even be deemed wisest to avoid this question regarding the receiving of the Holy Spirit, which seems to most men to carry them into mystical and vague regions where they are not at home. Why can we not be satisfied with the plain practical matter of seeing what is the Christian thing to do and doing it? What more can be needed than to trust God as our Father and to try to follow Jesus Christ? Let a man talk to us about applying Christian principles to business and society and we have before us something that is difficult but definite and comprehensible. Let him begin to talk about " receiving the Holy Spirit " and we feel ourselves getting lost as though in a dense fog.

This vagueness and indefiniteness may be due, not to the nature of the conception of the Holy Spirit, but to the absence from our experience of the reality of the Spirit. In reading we come upon pages or even whole books where the meaning, in spite of our best efforts, remains vague and confused in our minds. Later when we re-read these books every word may convey its full measure of meaning. The obscurity lay in ourselves and

not in the thought of the author. Thus, the emptiness of
these words " Holy Spirit," and the uneasy feeling they
give us, may be an indication of a blind spot in our religion. We are grazing the surface of a truth which one
day may appear to us as the truth without which all the
rest of our religion remains unintelligible and sterile.
The fact that the Holy Spirit seems not indispensable
to Christian living, and that we have a tendency to avoid
the subject, may be the best possible proof that at this
point has occurred our most serious neglect of the truth
of the Gospel. We cannot avoid Paul's embarrassing
question; it searches us; and few will be bold enough to
answer at once with a confident and positive affirmative.

Christian references to a Spirit of God sometimes
meet with the criticism that it is high time men ceased
looking for a supernatural power to do that which will
never be done until men themselves do it. John Dewey,
the American philosopher, repudiates all belief in the
supernatural because he is convinced that in it men are
shifting *their* duty and responsibility onto a power *not
themselves* which they hope will make for righteousness.
To deny that this happens constantly among Christians
is impossible. One often hears prayers for a regeneration
of the Church by an outpouring of the Holy Spirit from
men who are giving neither their minds nor their spirits
to the difficult disciplines through which alone God
can regenerate his Church. It is hard at times to keep

back the impetuous words, " How dare you pray for the
Spirit and put the responsibility on God for his work not
being done when the real hindrance to its accomplish-
ment is in you, not in God? " But even the philosopher
has overreached himself when he denies the possibility
of a supernatural power in the universe which may work
through man and multiply the efficacy and fruitfulness
of his endeavors. Like all Christian beliefs, that belief
may be so falsified that it becomes a hindrance to righteousness, a snare and a delusion. Surely, however, it is
illogical to condemn the belief itself because false and
undesirable forms of it appear.

One would think that the world's recent experiences
with electricity would have made men slow to deny the
possibility of great resources of spiritual power in the
universe. When the suggestion was first made that there
existed vast unused stores of electrical power which
could be brought into the service of man, there were
many who were skeptical and called it an impractical
dream. They were not interested in exploring such remote possibilities. They were content to continue in the
plain way of doing things to which they had been accustomed all their lives. Electricity seemed too vague
and mysterious for practicality. But today we marvel
only that this power which does so much for us should
have been here in the universe untouched and unused
through thousands and thousands of years. Why, then,

should it be difficult for us to conceive of an inexhaustible store of *spiritual* energy and power and life at the heart of things, unexplored indeed by most men, and yet capable, if let loose through human life, of working as great transformations spiritually in the world as electricity has achieved in a material way?

The Prophets and Jesus

In the Old Testament there are numerous references to the Spirit of God as a creative power and as the agency through which the Divine touches and affects human life. The prophets speak under the inspiration of the Spirit of God, claiming for their words the authority of God himself. But nowhere in the Old Testament do individuals say that they have " received " the Holy Spirit in the sense of the presence and power of God actually dwelling in a human life. That claim belongs peculiarly to the New Testament. Joel looked for the day when God would pour out his Spirit upon all flesh as a time when there would begin a great new age. In John the Baptist the longing for this baptism of the Spirit becomes an eager and confident expectation. John was a great prophet, an agent in the hand of God to rouse sluggish consciences and to turn people back to God and righteousness. No one would dare to say that he was without the Spirit of God. Yet he himself was certain that there was a fullness of the knowledge and power of God into which neither he nor any who had come before him had been able to enter. He was in travail of soul for the coming of that Spirit which, he expected, would bring a new humanity.

The original account of the baptism of Jesus, as also of his temptations, may be taken as resting upon Jesus' own description of what happened. Thus when it is said that in the baptism the Holy Spirit descended upon Jesus, we must give the words their full significance, taking them to mean that at that time there came into being a relationship between Jesus and the Spirit of God which had not formerly been realized. Jesus was filled with the Spirit, and it was in the power of this Spirit that he was enabled to live the life and do the mighty works that he did from that time on. Men in contact with him were conscious of an overwhelming power working through him. When he healed men, it was the power of the Lord which was present to heal. When his teachings searched the hearts of his hearers and wrought conviction, they said that his word was " with power."

Today it is the style to explain the marvelous accomplishments of Jesus by reference to the attributes of his character and personality. Jesus would never have permitted this praise of himself. He would have attributed everything from beginning to end to the wisdom and power of the Spirit of God dwelling in him. But with

Jesus, as with all men, his relationship with the Spirit of God was a personal relationship. The Spirit was not an impersonal Divine something which became an unconditional possession even with him. It was a fellowship sustained by prayer which needed for its preservation those quiet hours when he withdrew himself from his disciples.

The most significant passage for Jesus' teaching concerning the Holy Spirit is the interview with Nicodemus in the third chapter of The Gospel According to St. John. Nicodemus, who is as fine an example of spirituality and virtue as could be produced by any of our civilizations, hears from the lips of Jesus the demand for a new humanity. Spirituality and virtue are not enough; revision and reformation of the old religious ideals will not meet the need. A new kind of humanity must come into being if the new world is to become an actuality. Nicodemus, staggered by this setting in question of all that he has counted his religion, asks how this can be. That it ought to be he does not question, but that such a new humanity can actually displace the old humanity which he knows by long experience, he is unable to believe.

The same difficulty emerges in each new assertion of the impossibility of living out under human conditions the principles of Jesus. They are too far beyond our human powers, we hear; although wonderful ideals of what life ought to be, they are impractical for men who have to live their lives in the real world. Jesus would agree that this is true. He knew that man as man is incapable of the life of the Kingdom of God. He who enters into it must live, not by his own wisdom and power, but with all the wisdom and power of the Spirit of God opened to him and flooding in upon him. Only thus is the new humanity possible.

Shirley Jackson Case, in an essay on Christian ethics, asserts that it ought to be possible to divorce the ethics of Jesus from all matters of doctrine and all relation to his Person, and to consider them purely as the explication of a way of life which any man may choose to follow. What he wants is what many would like to have, the Christian way of living completely free from all bother about deeper religious considerations. Jesus' plain assertion is that this is an impossibility. It is, in brief, a desire to have God's salvation without God. Christian living becomes possible only through the fellowship of the Holy Spirit. When Christian ethics are divorced from the Person of Christ, and man in his own power attempts the application of them in every realm of life, the result invariably is that the ethics applied turn out to be something other than Christian — the rather praiseworthy ethics of Nicodemus perhaps, or of Plato, or of modern intellectualism, but not the ethics of Jesus. Jesus' own conviction was that the life he held before men as their true life is an impossibility except for those who are " born of the Spirit," or, to use Paul's phrase, those who have " received the Holy Spirit."

The Early Church

Characteristic of the whole Early Christian Church was the emphasis placed upon the Spirit. We are told of the disciples' receiving the Spirit when the risen Saviour breathed upon them. Then at Pentecost the Spirit of God seemed to sweep through the whole multitude. Luke, seeking to put into words the overpowering might of that experience, uses physical terms to describe it — " a sound from heaven as of a rushing mighty wind," tongues of flame. As though the dykes of heaven had burst, the streams of heavenly influences were flooding down into the lives of these men. Or perhaps it would be truer to say that the dykes of heaven are always open. What happened at Pentecost was that the hearts and lives of these men were opened wide for the Spirit of God in all his fullness to come in upon them and take them captive for himself and for his Kingdom.

We marvel at the vitality of the faith of the early Christians and at the rapidity with which their Church grew and spread to other lands. We know that as men they possessed at the beginning few qualifications that would lead us to expect great achievements. The immediate disciples of Jesus were not well-educated men, nor do they seem to have been highly talented. As the Gospels portray them, they appear to have been very ordinary men. They were hardly the type a modern organizer would choose if he desired to make a whirlwind success of any movement. Paul says of Christians in general that not many wise, not many mighty, not many noble are called. God has chosen the foolish, the weak, the mean and despised. These men did not set out to transform the world because of any confidence in their natural abilities.

We know what they accomplished, the triumphs which they wrought, the Churches which they established, the transformations of manners and morals which they effected. The creation of the New Testament in less than a century of Christianity was in itself a monumental achievement. When we ask the reason for this superabundant vitality and fruitfulness of the Apostolic Church, it is all traced to the outpouring of the Spirit of God. They went forward drawing upon resources of wisdom and truth and spiritual power far beyond all that they possessed in themselves. The triumphs were not theirs but God's.

Paul

Nowhere in the New Testament are references to the Spirit so frequent as in the letters of Paul. For him, Christianity was a life in the power of the Spirit or it was nothing. Since we have evidence concerning the religious life of the pre-Christian Paul, we have the opportunity of comparing in him the good, religious life without the Spirit and the good, religious life with the Spirit. Paul is the man to whom we should put our questions: " Why can we not be content with goodness and religiousness? Why must there be a receiving of the Spirit? "

Paul in his old Jewish life was a man of strong religious character. He was not only devoted to his religion, but was intent upon excelling in the service of it and in the punctilious observance of its duties. Among us he would be respected and honored as an outstandingly fine character and a pillar of religion. Were any man today to live a life such as Paul lived as a Jew, it would be deemed unreasonable and overcritical to suggest that there was any serious lack in his piety. Yet Paul himself tells us that in those days something was seriously wrong in his inner life. It was all strain and conflict without any deep satisfaction. The good life was a burden to him, just as it is a burden to many Christians today if they would admit the truth. Paul learned what every man must learn, that the surest road to misery and despair is to pledge one's soul to high ideals and have only one's own natural strength and wisdom and character with which to strive toward them.

In Christ, Paul found the solution of this central problem of his life. He was pledged now to a way of life far higher and more difficult than that which had tortured him before with its unattainableness. More clearly than ever before he recognized the power of the forces of evil both within himself and working upon him from without. He knew that to the end of time he would be of the earth earthy, that the battle of the spirit against the flesh would have to go on without ceasing. Now, however, he fought, not as in a doubtful battle, but with the assurance of victory. The essential victory had been won through what Christ had accomplished in his life and in his death, and Paul's own immediate victory was being won through God's Spirit dwelling in him, the power of God himself working in him. He did not dissolve the moral dilemma, the tension between what is and what ought to be, by escaping into mysticism. He did not reduce his standards and accommodate them to his natural potentialities as so many do. God's Spirit brought to him the earnest of a new and undreamed-of synthesis of life. His indwelling presence made him a new creature, created in him a new humanity, and enabled him to find in his present experience the life and peace and joy of the Kingdom of God.

The Holy Spirit Confronts Us with the Ultimate Decision of Faith

Belief in God, the Holy Spirit, is belief in a living God who can actually enter into our present world as the decisive factor of existence. The world and life are so constituted that at the central point upon which all things depend there is a void. At times in our lives we come up to the very edge of it, and, peering in, are shaken to the depths of our souls by the helplessness of our humanity at the very point where our need is greatest. Mankind in these present years has been looking into that void, with a resultant spread of hopelessness and despair about the world's future. Although we try to formulate solutions, both secular and religious, that will bridge it over, our bridges are all too short. But do we consider the possibility that that void at the center is meant in the nature of things to be there, that it is the vacancy in existence which only God can fill, the hole in the center of the wheel which must be left clear for the axle if the wheel is ever to turn? Our supreme godlessness is that we try of ourselves to fill that void; we try to put ourselves into the vacancy and to achieve a life in which we shall not need God, except, perhaps, as a necessary quantity to complete our intellectual and emotional world. There is room in our world view for a

God, but not for a living God who is a real power in the
world and enters into the present hour as its all-determining factor!

It is of the utmost significance that the outpouring of
the Holy Spirit in the Early Church was followed by an
experiment in communal living. The experiment may
justly be said to have resulted in failure. Communal living was found to attract too many lazy folk into the
Christian fold, people whose one desire was to live out
of the general fund. But behind the experiment we must
recognize a remarkable phenomenon. The possessive
instinct was so completely quelled in a large group of
people that they were willing to surrender their private
and personal rights in property. We know how powerful that instinct is from the cradle to the grave, and to it
in its exaggerated expression we trace most of the economic troubles of the world. Let the selfish acquisitiveness of man he subdued and an equally powerful concern
for the common good take its place, and what marvelous possibilities would lie before us!

Men say that that is only a dream, a hopeless dream.
Human nature will never permit its realization. In that
they are partly right, for human nature is intrinsically
egotistical and even the highest human standards leave
the acquisitiveness of man only slightly curbed. But they
do not consider the possibility of a transformation of
human nature. For them it is as a fixed quantity. Among

these early Christians who claim to have " received the Holy Spirit " there appears, however, a new kind of human nature. The ego is gone from the center, selfish possessiveness has been severely curbed if not broken, and the dominant thought is for the good of all. All that has happened is that God has become a reality in these people's lives. They have given him his place at the center of life and have accepted their own true place in relationship to him. They have become humble stewards of all the good things of life, administering them no longer for themselves alone but for the glory of God and the good of their fellows.

God the Father Almighty, God who for our sakes dwelt in Jesus Christ, comes to us and abides with us in the Holy Spirit. It is wrong to think of the Spirit as a kind of detached spiritual essence scattered through humanity, as a divine spirit working here, there, and everywhere, quite apart from the Lord in whose hands we are and from the Saviour who redeems us. Through the Spirit, God the Father Almighty ceases to be merely the object of our thoughts, a distant fatherly Being, and becomes the Father with whom we live day by day as children of his household. Through the Spirit, Christ the Word no longer exists for us merely in the documents of ancient records, but becomes God speaking to us in the immediate situation of today, that we may live and not die. It is the same God and the same Christ who come to us in the Holy Spirit and ask that we should let our whole lives become temples for them to dwell in.

Thus, the question of the Holy Spirit brings every part of our Christian faith to an issue. We realize that we are not just being asked to believe certain propositions concerning the nature of God and concerning Jesus Christ, and perhaps concerning some other related matters. We are being asked nothing less than that God himself who came into the world in Jesus Christ should be allowed to come into *our* world and upon the scene of life today *in us*. The chief obstacle in the way of God's salvation is our unwillingness that that should happen. We want to believe in him at a safe distance, not in the dangerous and almost terrifying closeness of the Holy Spirit. We do not want to believe in a God who will actually take possession and control of our entire life. To speak of the Holy Spirit and to know what we speak of is to be confronted with the ultimate decision of faith. The issue is joined — God or self — and there can be no compromise.

Chapter 8

The Church of Christ

EVERY matter of belief is an urgent one. This book has failed in one of its primary aims if it has not made clear that beliefs and life are inextricably interwoven, that we are what we believe. We cannot examine a question of belief as we would a problem in algebra, looking at it in complete detachment. The objectivity of detachment is impossible in religion because our lives are bound up with the questions, and the discovery of truth is always the discovery of our true life. Thus, it is not a delight in abstract discussions which makes us venture into the field of doctrine, but rather the conviction that we cannot conduct our lives upon a thoroughly Christian basis until we know with clearness what we believe. We trace the prevalent confusion in religious life back to its source in the confusion and chaos of religious beliefs.

The Peril of Our Present Situation

The subject of the Church has in it, however, a special urgency today because of the situation in which the

Church finds itself. The Protestant Church of our time is very much like a house standing in the midst of the floodwaters of a great river. The swirling waters break against it, and the storms shake it. As we watch, we see walls crumbling here and there and disappearing under the flood. We ask: " Can it stand against every storm? Will its foundations be strong enough to hold? " But we do not ask our questions as men standing in safety on the bank of the swollen stream would ask them. The earnestness and urgency of our concern is that we dwell *within* that house, and our fate is bound up with the fate of it.

In Russia, a Church which had centuries of hallowed traditions, which maintained itself in magnificent fashion, and which seemed to all observers to have a powerful hold upon the common people, in a short period of time was brought down into ruins. The startling thing was not that the Russian Church went down before the onslaught of Communism, but that so few seemed to care that it was gone. We feel an uneasiness about what would happen to our Church under similar circumstances. Once let Christianity cease to be respectable, let it become socially and politically disapproved among us, and then let anyone answer whether or not the Church in our land would survive better than did the great Russian Church.

In Germany, the Church is experiencing critical days.

The impression given by the newspapers during the pre-war days was that all that happened in the Churches was the direct result of an attempt by the Nazi Government to whip them into line with its regime. It was pictured as simply a coercing of Christianity by Hitler. Were that true, the situation would be less serious than it is.

The alarming truth is that the movement to put the Protestant Church in Germany into subjection to the Nazi State began *in the Church itself*. A mystic faith in the nation, a passionate and unreasoning patriotism, became so mingled with religious faith that men, some of them Christian leaders of high intelligence and fine character, were unable to hold the two apart. " Christ *and* the Nation " became the watchword of the day. Few men realized that the inevitable result would be the enslavement of Christ and his people to the nation, rather than of the nation to Christ. There is a faithful remnant which maintained and still maintains the sole sovereignty of Christ over his Church, refusing to compromise with any other authority. These few refuse to vow unconditional allegiance to Hitler because their only unconditional allegiance is to Jesus Christ. Their contention is that the more loyal the Church is to its Founder, the greater and the nobler will be its contribution to the life of the nation. They stand for a holy Church, and are willing to die for it, should the need

arise. It is clear, then, that the terrible situation in which
Protestantism in Germany finds itself arose directly out
of the uncertainty of Christians as to where the Church
should stand in relation to the life of a people. The
hour of testing merely brought to light the hidden
weakness which had long been there.

Today the name of Martin Niemoeller is known
round the world, and Christians everywhere have
thrilled at the tales of a new age of heroic Christianity
which have come out of Germany, Norway, and Hol-
land. Yet there is a real danger that the Church in our
land may be too quick in encouraging itself with these
instances of an impregnable Church. It has been written
for us to read, in letters each of which has been shaped
at terrific cost of suffering by Christian men and women,
that a Church that is true to its nature has a strength to
resist evil that belongs to no merely human institution.
But we should take much thought before we assert that
our Churches, as they are, are such a Church. First we
should look carefully at the Churches and Christians in
those lands that have *not* stood in the time of testing but
have *fallen,* and let ourselves be disturbed by the close
parallels between their former attitudes and those which
prevail in wide sections of our Churches.

It is an axiom today that Protestantism in its fundamental characteristics is remarkably similar in all lands.
The tendencies and influences that have shaped modern

Protestantism have acknowledged no limitation of national barriers. Individual situations may vary in details, but when a Continental or a British Protestant discusses his problems, the Canadian or American Protestant recognizes those problems as his own. Therefore, we can expect to find the same weaknesses in us which were brought to light by the day of decision in the German Church. When two families are living in similar houses alongside each other and one house comes crashing down with disastrous consequences, the inhabitants of the second house will be impelled to seek at once for dangerous faults in their own foundations. The state of the Christian Church among us does not justify confidence and assurance any more than did the state of the German Church. We can take no lofty and superior self-righteous attitude, for there is the same uncertainty among us concerning the true nature of the Church. Would any man who knows the Church from the inside assert that there is less of falsity and error, less of self-seeking and Pharisaism, less of superficial nostrums, less of a nationalized Christianity, in our Churches than in theirs? The weaknesses which proved almost fatal for them are our weaknesses too. The only difference is that we live farther down the river, and the flood which overwhelmed them is not yet close enough for us to see its danger.

If we look along our walls, we may detect evidences of the waters already rising, quietly but steadily. There is a strong element of definite antagonism to the Church in the intellectual atmosphere of our day. Many of the apostles of modern knowledge — biologists, astronomers, philosophers, psychologists, historians, literary men — seem to regard the reconstruction of religion as a task for which their training has fitted them peculiarly. They pronounce upon religious subjects with a dogmatism and assurance which they would condemn heartily in any theologian. Their common presupposition is that historic Christianity is done for. Some naïvely propose substitutes, their ideas of what would be an adequate religion for an intelligent man of today. Their influence, however, remains largely negative. The pressure of this point of view in universities and schools, having the authority of eminent men of learning behind it, has had devastating effects upon the religious faith of young people in their formative years. It has created, and is creating, a community in which a large part of the better educated people regard themselves as emancipated from the Christian faith, and in their mild and superior agnosticism would quite willingly sit by and see the Christian Church die. The witness of their lives is decidedly *against* the Christian Church. Were some radical issue to arise in our society, we might well discover that this intellectual antagonism had hardened into a practical rejection of the Christian Church.

Then from underneath comes the cry against the

Church that it is an instrument of the upper, comfortable classes, used by them in order to keep themselves on top and to drug into submission all who might cause trouble for the existing order of society. The sharpness of that criticism is that there is so much truth in it, though few who are involved are conscious that they are making this use of the Church. Think of the contrast between the people who form the average Christian congregation and the people among whom Jesus chose to have his ministry. Would the poor and the outcasts and the sinners that gathered around Jesus feel very much at home in our Churches? And if not, why not? Has not the Church tended increasingly to become an association for religious purposes of the people of the middle and upper classes of society? That characteristic in the Church accounts for much of the growing antagonism from beneath.

Most disturbing of all should be the fact that many who count themselves members of the Church no longer really believe in the Church of Jesus Christ. They believe perhaps in the necessity of a religious institution to take care of the so-called spiritual aspect of life in the community. Every decent community needs Churches just as it needs schools and other municipal services. As good citizens, they feel a responsibility to provide for the Church, but as long as it seems to be carried on in an adequate fashion they are content. They are aware of a need that somewhere instruction in the virtues should be dispensed. Children and many adults need such instruction, and they are concerned that it should be provided. But the greater their own consciousness of virtue, the less do they feel that they themselves need to be submitted to the ministrations of the Church.

Actually, such Churchmen are not interested in Christianity at all, if by Christianity we mean Christian discipleship, but only in religion and morals, and in these they are interested only in that degree which seems necessary to keep the world they know steady and sane and congenial. Even the upheaval of the present day, with its threat to the security of their world, has served only to make them a little more religious and slightly more concerned about moral questions. Nothing is truer of our Church of today than that most people in it have not the slightest concern about discipleship. That the Church is being used to serve *their* purposes, and that it is not serving the purposes for which it was founded, does not trouble them in the least. They pass over, as though they had never been written, all the conditions laid down by Jesus concerning those who would be called by his name. The fact is that they do not believe in the Church as it was founded by Jesus Christ, and consciously or unconsciously they have molded it into a form which is more in accordance with their own desires and conceptions. What looks like indifference is actually unbelief. Were

the Church suddenly to stand forth in its true nature
with sharpness, and with something of its original offen-
siveness, this unbelief might crystallize into savage antagonism.

Because our Church doors are still open, and the society in which we live treats us in general with courtesy;
because we can still on occasion make a considerable
show of external strength and have statistics to prove
that in spite of all semblances of death we are still alive,
it is hard for us to grasp the seriousness of our present
situation. We see problems and weaknesses, but we do
not see that it is a matter of life and death. Neither did
the Churches in other lands, until the blow had fallen.

What Is the Church?

The question we must attempt to answer is, What is
the Church? — a question which at first sight may not
seem particularly difficult. The church is that building
with the spire pointing toward heaven where you go on
Sundays to worship, or to dream. The Church is the sum
total of a multitude of organizations ranging all the way
from badminton clubs to prayer meetings. It is the society of people, young and old, who center their lives
as Christians around this building, some of them good
people and some of them not so good. The Church is the
historic institution, of which we are but a small part,

which stretches across this land from Atlantic to Pacific and sends out its branches into other lands. But we cannot stop there with our definitions. The Church consists of many historic institutions in all countries, with a membership of hundreds of millions, differing widely in their practices and beliefs but held together by the one common bond, the name " Christian."

When we have said all that, we still have not begun to say what the Church of Jesus Christ is in its essence. We have described an external structure and an external society and organization which have come to be what they are through a variety of influences, not all of them by any means Christian. But this Church that we see and know is not of itself the Church in which we believe. Belief in the Church does not mean the acceptance of the existing order of things that constitutes the Church. More often, when we look into the life of the Church, we have to say, not, " This is the Church of Christ," but, " This is what the Church of Christ ought not to be." In our minds we have the thought of another Church and in our hearts the longing for another Church, which, we know, could come into existence if we would let it. We are conscious, painfully conscious, of the great gulf between the Church as it is and the Church as it ought to be.

Jesus, with only his own most intimate disciples before him, saw two possibilities for the Church which they were to form. He said to them, " Ye are the light of the world." Immediately he went on to speak of a candle, lighted and burning, but senselessly placed under a bushel measure where it could serve no one. Again he said, " Ye are the salt of the earth," but, still looking at them and speaking to them, he went on to describe a salt which had lost its savor and thereby was deprived of all that gave it effectiveness and value in the world: " It is thenceforth good for nothing, but to be cast out, and to be trodden under foot of men." In which of these likenesses do we recognize the closest resemblance to our Church and to our individual lives as Christians — the concentrated salt which gives sharpness and taste to everything, or the insipid mass which has no saltiness left in it; the candle on the candlestick which gives light to all that are in the room, or the lighted candle stupidly set away under a basket? We are none too quick to answer, for there is doubt in our minds where we belong. Is it not a judgment upon our Church and upon us that there should be that element of uncertainty as to which likeness suits us best? The boldness to assert that we are the light of the world, that we are the salt of the earth, that we are the true Church, does not seem to be ours.

What, then, is the nature of this true Church which we are not, but for which we long and pray, as men who have been watching in weariness all night reach out toward the dawn? Two words describe its entire nature:

Jesus Christ. That and nothing less than that is what the Church is meant to be — a body of people in whom Jesus Christ himself lives again to work his works, to speak his words, and to feed the souls of men. Perhaps out of a false sense of reverence for Jesus we have not dared to make this equation in which alone the true magnitude of the Church's task comes to light. Jesus said, " I am the light of the world," but he said also, " Ye are the light of the world."

There is no need for contradiction or confusion between these two statements. The same truth emerges in Paul's words, " Ye are the body of Christ." Jesus' body was the means whereby he was able to enter into the stream of human history and touch men's lives for a few short years. But that body was nailed to a cross, and the last breath of life passed from it. Then, when he had risen from the grave, Jesus began to take to himself a new body. The members of it he chose where he pleased, one in Jerusalem, another on the Damascus road, a third in Athens, and a fourth in Rome. He had to have a human body, responsive to every bidding of his spirit, if he was to continue his work among men. With this new body, he had the advantage over the old of being able to be in a thousand, or even a million places, at one time. Sometimes the Spirit of Jesus is regarded as working in the world quite apart from all human instrumentality. We are not so unwise as to say that that is impossible. In the New Testament, however, that was *not* the mode of the activity of the risen Christ. He required human lives to be molded into a body for him, and through such a body he wrought his triumphs. Paul said, " I live; yet not I, but Christ liveth in me." That was the reality of the Church. Today the Church is a true Church only in so far as Christ actually lives in it.

Whenever men have turned away disillusioned and disheartened from the Church, has not the reason often been that they have met with a spirit there which was not the spirit of Jesus Christ? Even in the severest criticisms and condemnations of the Church, we must often recognize an incoherent longing for the true Church. When we come to consider the problem of the multitudes who, in spite of all our efforts, persistently refuse to come into our Churches, must we not entertain the possibility that the fault is ours, that they do not come because they do not find Jesus Christ in our Churches?

The usual practice is to speak rather harshly of the ungodliness and spiritual degeneracy of the unchurched masses. We good Church people look down our noses at them disapprovingly, and we are never done scolding them and expressing our horror at them. We organize revivals in the hope that they may come inside and let themselves be converted. We talk, until we are weary of talking, about ways and means of carrying the Church to these people. And we get nowhere. All our efforts are doomed to failure because we refuse to recognize the source of the difficulty. The body of Christian people with whom they come into contact day by day does not show itself to them as indubitably the body of Christ. It is not the voice of Christ they hear speaking to them either in rebuke or in promise, and it is not the spirit of Christ which they feel meeting them in their dealings with us. Because there is something inconclusive about our Christianity, the world is not convinced. If men could see plainly in us that the Christian life is an abundant, overflowing life, a life that is like a light shining in the world — if men could see Jesus Christ in us — either they would be eager to come into fellowship with us and share the fullness of the life of the Kingdom or they would hate us for what we are. They would not remain indifferent as they do.

The center of Christ's being was redemptive love. The passion of his life was to bring men out of the loneliness and helplessness of themselves into a free, open life with God and with their fellow men. For that he lived and died. Yet what place has redemptive love of that kind in the activities and life of our Churches and in our lives as individual Christians? How near the center is it? And how often is it a passion in us? If we could even see the gap which lies between his thoughts and our thoughts, his ways and our ways, it would be the first step toward a new health in the Church. We can talk as we like about setting Christ at the center; unless redemptive love is the central and all-determining motive of the Church's life, we have no share in Christ. The application of that truth might have some drastic practical effects upon the present-day order of things in the average congregation.

Few Christians even consider it possible for the love that dwelt in Christ to dwell in them. Redemptive love! That is the nature of God and the glorious nature of Christ, they say, but not the nature of man. Man belongs on another level. Yes, but Jesus Christ came down to the level of man's life for this express purpose, that the love which is God's own nature should be shed abroad in human hearts and should begin to become man's nature. We stand in wonder at the thought, and we ask, " How can this be? " It is too high for us. But " the wind bloweth where it listeth." If we are ready and willing, it can be. Were we to let it do so, the love of Christ could possess our natures from this day forth. Should that truly happen in us and in our fellow Christians, would not the Church then in truth be the salt of the earth and the light of the world?

The Church in which we believe is the Church which is the body of Christ. This and this alone is the Church which has the promise that all that the world can do against it will be in vain. Churches die, not from outward pressure, but from inward rot. The only real danger which we need fear is that Christ should cease to dwell in us, for that alone can bring us to ruin. That statement has important consequences. If it is true, then our first duty is not to combat secularism or Communism or any of the philosophies of life which seem to threaten the Church. That duty may come later, but our first and inescapable duty is that we should submit everything in the life of the Church and in our religious viewpoints to a constant, intense, and thoroughly critical scrutiny, that we may detect at once wherein *we* go aside from Christ. Our one sure defense is trueness to Christ in thought, word, and deed. Jesus' promise to the Church, as with joy he saw it already embodied in Peter and the other disciples, is his promise to every Church that makes him sovereign in all its life and work: " The gates of hell shall not prevail against it."

Clearly, then, belief in the Church does not mean an acceptance of the Church as it is, but rather an acceptance which has in it also a rejection. Because the Church in which we believe is the body of Christ, we are forced to be intensely and unremittingly critical of the Church as we find it in the world. Men who adopt a " standpat " attitude and decry all criticism of the Church usually pose as models of loyalty and devotion. They are in reality disloyal. They are substituting loyalty to a worldly organization for loyalty to the body of Christ. The adoption of a critical attitude may well be a sign, not of a weakening, but of a strengthening of our devotion to the Church. Criticism from outside, which measures the Church by worldly standards and finds it wanting, is always destructive and leads men away from the Church. But criticism, even the most radical, which insists upon holding against the walls of the Church the measuring line, which is Jesus Christ, should be encouraged and given the freest scope, for by its nature it leads the minds of men, not away from, but toward the Church. Paul's words are very apt for the Church today: " If we would judge ourselves, we should not be judged." Instead of lamenting and combating the storms of criticism which rage against us, we should be taking up in earnest the humbling and exacting task of self-criticism.

Thus we see that the article of the creed, " I believe in . . . the holy Catholic Church," cannot stand alone. It is comprehensible only in the light of the preceding articles, and is the direct consequence of them. If we believe in Jesus Christ as the Saviour of the world, and if we believe in the Holy Spirit as the Spirit of God which can create in us today the very life and work of Jesus Christ, then already we believe in the Church. That and nothing less than that is the true Church, an association of people in whom God by his Spirit causes Jesus Christ to be reborn. In spite of the fact that they remain sinners, he lives and works and speaks through them in our present-day world, using them as a body for himself.

This Church is catholic. It is always one. The body of Christ cannot be divided. That may sound contrary to fact, for is it not divided into Presbyterian, Anglican, United, Baptist, Lutheran, and so forth? We have heard much in recent years about these " sore wounds in the body of Christ." But is a man necessarily divided from his friend by the mere fact that he lives in one house and his friend lives in another? Not at all. Neither is there any reason why the unity of the body of Christ need be disturbed by the fact that the community of Christian people is divided into a number of families. There are reasons which may rightly be urged for the preservation of particular families of Christians, at least for a time, because of distinctive contributions which they can make to the whole. But that need provide no barrier to fellowship and Christian unity. True fellowship overleaps all external barriers. We must be ready to recognize and to own the presence of the true Church wherever it manifests itself, regardless of the name by which it is called.

Protestantism in recent years has manifested a great concern about the unity of the Church. One thinks of the movements for the consolidation of separate

Churches — in England, Scotland, Germany, Canada, the United States, and in yet other countries — which have occupied a large place in the minds of leading Churchmen of the last generation. One thinks also of the ecumenical movement which, by a series of world conferences and by an opening of the channels of information and fellowship between Church and Church, has given to the Protestant Churches a new sense of being one Church. The fact that in the past four years, when our world has fallen apart, the world Church has not fallen apart, but has maintained a fellowship which reaches across all barriers of nation and race, has made a deep impression upon the minds of Christians everywhere.

In these various movements, though all of them seem to have to do with unity, we must draw a necessary distinction. There are two impulses at work, often in a single movement, impulses which are quite different in origin, nature, and consequences. The one is a passion for the unification of the visible Church, arising from the conviction that the Christian Church will have strength in the face of the unbelieving world only when it is able to present a completely united front. The serious divisions are therefore *those which show in the Church's structure.*

The other is a concern which, beginning with the conviction that the Church *is* one in Jesus Christ — that there can be only one body of Christ, only one chosen people of God — seeks to open up lines of communication and to establish means of fellowship and co-operation in order that Christians in all the world, regardless of race or Church tradition, may realize and confess their oneness. The serious divisions, from this standpoint, are *those which keep us from being one in faith*. The real tragedy is that in spite of our common use of Christian terminology, different faiths and even contradictory faiths are operative among us.

Those impelled by the former impulse tend to minimize all differences in regard to faith and doctrine, and refuse to admit their implications or even to take them with real seriousness, because their great eagerness is for a unity which will impress the world outside the Church. They push impatiently both for a statement of the things on which we are agreed and for an immediate organic unification on the basis of such a statement.

On the other hand, those who are actuated by the latter impulse are hesitant about organic unifications, because they regard all matters concerning the external structure of the Church as secondary, and because they are convinced that the world is to be redeemed not by the impressiveness of the Church's organization but by the trueness of the Church to its nature as the very body of Jesus Christ. They believe that the first task to which we who call ourselves Christians should address ourselves is that of speaking to each other honestly and frankly, and together pressing the inquiry as to why our message to the world is not one but several, why it is confused and contradictory, and why the principles which determine our attitudes and actions are likewise confused. Going farther, this group recognize that the tallying of points of agreement may be deceptive, covering over an issue which, although it appears only at one point, actually creates a divergence at all points. There comes to mind a book written by a competent theologian of the German Christian Church, nine tenths of which sounded like intelligent evangelical Christianity. In the other tenth a turn was given to the whole argument which made it a theological justification of compromise with the Nazi State and a basis for Church action which we can regard as nothing less than a betrayal of the Church of Jesus Christ.

It is important that the distinction between these two impulses, both concerned with unity, should be recognized. Both are operative in the ecumenical movement, and many of its leaders seem unconscious of the essential divergence of intention. It should be made clear that belief in the unity of the Church of Christ does not necessarily commit us to an approval of any and every program of practical unification which may be brought forward.

The Church Is a Mission

Finally, belief in the Church involves necessarily belief in evangelical missions. The man who considers the Church indispensable in his own community and yet dispensable in Chinese or African communities is queerly illogical. The only explanation is that he does not believe in Jesus Christ, the Saviour of the world, but in a religion which he calls Christianity. He is not interested in a Church which is the body of Christ; a religious organization which maintains a decent level of morality, order, and spirituality in the community is enough. If in other countries there are religions with forces latent in them sufficient to do this, our part is to encourage them to produce their best, but we must refrain from interfering in their sphere of influence.

This point of view has been slipping into the minds of Christian people and has been undermining the missionary enterprise of our Churches. The presupposition is, of course, that an adequate life is possible apart from Jesus Christ. This contradicts the basic premises of the Christian faith and embodies a conception of religion that has no point of connection whatever with the New Testament. It is openly and frankly bent upon the abandonment of evangelical missions. But it cannot stop there. In this scheme of things there is no essential place for an evangelical Church at all. The next step, which some are already urging, is the abandonment by the Church of the New Testament Gospel, so that we may reform ourselves into a society for general culture, spirituality, and social uplift.

Nevertheless it may still be true that Jesus is the Light of the World. Perhaps, like the Pharisees, when we have reached our highest point of spirituality and righteousness, we still lack the one thing that is most necessary. We lack it just as did the Greeks, with all their culture, and as do the Chinese and Indian civilizations.

There is a life which man cannot know until he finds it in Christ, a life which is Christ being born again in us by faith and by the indwelling of the Spirit of God. If that life has become ours, there is that in its nature which compels us to send it on to others. It is not for us alone, but for all men. Christ belongs to the world, and we dare not keep him to ourselves. If we in our civilization need the Church, that in it Christ may live and speak, surely we cannot withhold that Church from other peoples merely because we recognize high values in the civilizations that are theirs. Civilizations and religions are not enough; the world needs Christ, and the Church should be the lowly channel through which Christ may come to the world in its need.

Chapter 9

The Forgiveness of Sins

LIKE THE DOCTRINE of the Church, that of the forgiveness of sins is dependent upon and inseparable from all that has gone before. It is not an experience apart and by itself, but a constituent part of all faith in God. Our Christian beliefs are empty imaginings of the mind and nothing more unless there is evident in our lives as their first and farthest-reaching fruit the forgiveness of our sins. What can we hear and understand of the Word of God unless by it the deafness is taken from our ears and the blindness from our eyes? That deafness and blindness we know to be one symptom of our sin, sin which dulls all our spiritual sensibility; therefore, to be given hearing ears and to have our sins forgiven are one and the same reality.

In relation to the God and Father who rules over all our days, forgiveness is the overcoming of our rebelliousness and the reconciling of our wills to his will for us. Who can say he believes in Jesus Christ unless he has been plunged into despair about the sinfulness of his own being by what he sees in Christ, and has then been lifted out of that sinfulness into a life of boundless hope by the word of pardon that Christ speaks to him?

The cross of Christ is the point in human history where all the defenses of our own righteousness and virtue are beaten down and we stand condemned, with Christ alone over against us. We see the enormity of our sin, that it crucifies love. Moreover, we see the omnipotence of love, that in its completest outpouring it establishes its indisputable sway over the heart of man.

When we think of the Holy Spirit, the word " Holy " at once tells us that the more fully the Spirit of God dwells in our lives, the more completely must all that is unholy pass from us. We cannot have God with us without having his holiness and his purity, and certainly we cannot have his holiness and his purity apart from the forgiveness of our sins.

The Church, as we saw in the preceding chapter, is the body of people who have found in Christ the forgiveness of their sins, who live daily by the grace of his pardon, and who, in the joy of the new life which is theirs, are seeking to open to all men, regardless of race or civilization, the possibility of a like pardon. The future life, with which we have yet to deal, has its highest meaning as the consummation of the work of forgiveness, the life of glory when sin and guilt shall be no more, when our blessedness will be that of perfect purity. It is impossible to touch the truth of Christianity at any point without finding ourselves confronted with the question of forgiveness. This breadth of the question must be kept in mind constantly, for far too often the scope of it has been narrowed and confined to a single element in experience, the pardoning of acts of wrong which have been done. It cannot be so confined. The roots of forgiveness are as deep as the nature of God himself and the sphere of its operation is as wide as human life.

Forgiveness Cannot Be Taken for Granted

It might seem at first sight an encouraging factor that Christian people have generally a firm assurance of the possibility of forgiveness. Looking more closely, we are disposed to see in that assurance merely a taking for granted of forgiveness. Voltaire once said: " God will forgive. It is his function to do so." The point of view of many Christians could not be expressed more exactly. They are Christians, and as such are confident that their God is merciful and forgiving. They are, therefore, not distressed about their sins. God will forgive and all will be well. But this belief in an easy forgiveness, which is undoubtedly the common view, must be branded as nothing more or less than immoral and paralyzing to the spiritual life. It is an attitude which must necessarily shut us out from the real presence and pardon of God. That will be evident at once if we consider a human parallel. Let us suppose that a man has done a wrong to one of his friends. The transgressor is blithely taking it for granted that his friend will forgive him. Indeed, so great is his confidence in his friend's leniency that he gives little thought to the wrong he has done. Would not that frame of mind in a man make it impossible for right relations to be restored between him and his friend? Yet, dare he take forgiveness for granted? If the wrong is to be passed over and treated as though it had not been, that is wholly in the hands of the person wronged and must come as a free and undeserved gift from him. If a man counts on that forgiveness as already his and acts as though it were, he shows himself not only unworthy of receiving but definitely *incapable* of receiving forgiveness.

Shall it be different, then, in our relationship with God? Dare we, with our sins upon us, face God with this easy confidence, taking it for granted that his forgiveness is already ours? Shall not an attitude which effectually bars us from the fellowship of man bar us also from the fellowship of God? It is not too much to say that this common frame of mind renders it impossible for God to forgive.

When forgiveness is taken for granted it becomes a subversive factor in the moral and spiritual life. We can think back over past experiences to a time or times when we have been severely tempted and remember when strong cords were drawing us into some pleasant sin. Conscience and desire were at war within us, desire enticing us into what we knew was wrong and knowledge of its wrongness barely holding us in check. Then there floated into the mind the thought that, after all, God would forgive us and remove any undesirable consequences. That thought, working dimly in the background of the mind, put an end to the soul's resistance. Perhaps trust in an easy forgiveness works more often unconsciously than consciously. At any rate it always destroys the integrity of conscience and weakens the whole moral fiber of a man. It is this that has caused so many eminent moral teachers to look with disfavor upon the idea of forgiveness. They have seen clearly that the man who is certain he will be forgiven all that he does wrongly, will no longer be in earnest about choosing what is right. Christian forgiveness never gives any man basis for such assurance; it can never be taken for granted.

Forgiveness is an act of God's free grace, and has no reality except as it is received each time anew as a gift from the hand of God. God may give it or he may withhold it. We can never count upon it. God writes no blank check of forgiveness even for the most soundly converted of Christians. Pardon must be *sought*. We must ask for it, with our whole soul rising up and asking, if we would receive it. If we would know the blessing of having it opened to us, we must knock, and keep on knocking, as humble suppliants at the door of God's mercy. God is not likely to be in earnest about granting us pardon until he sees that we are in earnest about our need for his pardon.

The Importance of Confession

Protestants are often heard making disparaging remarks about the Roman Catholic confessional or the practice of open confession in the Oxford Groups. Undoubtedly there are serious objections that may be raised against both. Yet one is inclined to ask such Protestants what *they* do about confession. The Catholics and the Groupers at least recognize that sins must be taken seriously and must be confessed if they are to be forgiven. In the minds of both is the salutary thought of the possibility that forgiveness may be withheld, of the possibility that even a professing Christian may remain unforgiven and therefore cursed by his sin. The commoner practice among Christian people is to assume that forgiveness is theirs without taking the trouble to make a detailed confession. They have a general confession of sin in their Sunday prayers and a formal request for forgiveness. However, they never get down to actual instances and tell God at what points in life and in what manner they have sinned and need forgiveness. There is no passion in their plea for forgiveness, for they begin with an assurance that they are already forgiven.

Confession of sin is simply a matter of becoming honest with God. We say to God that we have been living in a mist of self-delusion, drifting away ever farther from all knowledge of the truth about ourselves and about him. We recognize that there is much wrong in our personal life and in our relationships with others, and that all our unhappiness and unrest arises from that which is wrong. Dimly we know that until we get down to the bedrock of truth we shall never have any firm basis upon which to build our life.

At the same time we recognize the futility of an introverted self-examination. Our need is not to turn ourselves inside out and show all the seams. After all, that would not get us beyond our own judgment upon ourselves, which, in the nature of the case, since we are the prisoners at the bar, is hardly to be trusted. Our need is for God's judgment upon us — to see ourselves, not as others see us, but as God sees us. The question with which we begin is, What is the truth about my life as seen from the standpoint of God? " In thy light shall we see light." God's Word, especially as it sounds forth in the Person of Jesus Christ, must sound in our ears as a word of self-revelation, a word that brings us to ourselves, before we shall be prepared to confess our sins.

It is doubtful whether we should ever have courage to confess the full depths of our sin if we did not hear intermingled with the word that judges us the promise of pardon. The same word both casts us down and lifts us up. Knowledge of God and knowledge of sin belong together.

Let it be clear, then, that a man cannot bow the knee in prayer and, running his mind's eye quickly over the past day, make a confession of sins. True confession is possible only under the light of God's presence. We must ask God to show us where we have sinned and let him in our prayer lay bare to us our sin. Confession of sin is thus unlikely to be taken seriously by a person who is careless of God's revelation of himself in the Scriptures. In its full Christian sense it is, in fact, an impossibility for such a person. It is the knowledge of God which brings us to a consciousness of the truth about ourselves.

This suggests a criticism of both Catholic and Oxford Group confessionals. In spite of all efforts to the contrary, that which is likely to weigh most heavily in the mind of a Catholic is what the priest considers to be sin. That which is likely to shape the confession of an Oxford Grouper is what his fellow Groupers regard as sinful. Life remains within the circle of human standards, and is not brought out under the full, clear, penetrating light of God's own Word. What the priest sanctions and what the Group sanctions is not likely to be recognized as sinful. Yet these very things may be the most devastating sins of all, sins with the whole force of a religious society to support them.

Confession, whether it be made in the presence of human beings or not, is primarily a transaction between man and God. Man lays his life before God, asking that as the first boon of existence he should be shown the truth about himself. Confession is thus not a purely human act prior to forgiveness, but is an act of faith, possible only through the light of God's revealing Word and the inreaching of his Spirit by which he searches the heart.

Forgetting What Is Past Is Not Enough

There is a general reluctance today to deal with the subject of sin. It is regarded as a rather somber and depressing avenue of religious teaching which one should avoid if possible. The emphasis is upon the bright and happy and constructive elements in religion. We want a religion that cheers us up and helps us on our way. The demand is strong for sermons that will be glorified pep talks. To talk of sin is like introducing a death's-head at the feast of life. This mood is reinforced by the spread of a superficial type of popular psychology, according to which sin is a morbid idea that intelligent men should have discarded long ago. Of course, we are human and make mistakes, it is said, but we shall never get away from our mistakes by calling them sins and brooding over them. The healthy-minded man simply forgets his mistakes and goes on to the next phase of his life to see what he can make of it.

But the question which with reason may be asked is whether it is wise for the healthy-minded man to forget his mistakes if it is in the nature of things that his mistakes do not forget him. It may be that Paul, in saying, " Whatsoever a man soweth, that shall he also reap," is truer to the facts of life than are the modern enthusiasts for mental health. What we do and say and think enters into the web of our lives and becomes part of our selves. The past may in an external sense be gone never to return. Yet, in another sense, because it is *our* past it still lives in us and can exert a very great influence in determining our lives in the present and the future. Forgotten mistakes have a disconcerting way of coming back to visit when least expected. " Forget the past " is advice which is easy to give, but surely it is written plainly across the face of life that the past does not let itself be forgotten so easily. We may ignore the question of sin, but the question of sin will not ignore us.

There are lighthearted men who never concern themselves about such bothersome things as bills. As the bills come in, they toss them into the wastepaper basket, refusing to be troubled by them. They prefer to keep healthy, carefree minds. But one day such people find that their creditors have combined, and that the bailiff is at the door, ready to sell them out. So is it with our sins. We may dismiss them lightly. Nonetheless, they are there against us in life's outstanding accounts. The day is bound to come when they will combine against us, and we shall find ourselves on the brink of moral and spiritual ruin.

Moreover, it is wrong to describe a Christian man's concern with sin as a morbid and unhealthy brooding upon his mistakes. It is the mark of a Christian that he does *not* waste time and energy brooding over his sins, but takes them direct to God, where he finds pardon for them and has their weight lifted from him. The real Christian is the healthiest and happiest-minded man alive, because he has learned a way of dealing with his past which keeps it from being an obstruction to life in the present and future. The man who does the brooding is the man who, with a show of enlightenment, dismisses the idea of sin, while at the same time he grapples helplessly with things out of his own past which hold him enchained. He is like a man with a cinder in his eye, going about trying to look as though nothing were wrong, in distress but unable to seek help because he is unwilling to admit the presence of the cinder in his eye.

Not by any mere chance are the terms " God " and " sin " constantly associated together from beginning to end of the Bible. What the man of the Bible thinks of God makes it necessary for him to use the word " sin " as he looks into human life. Remove the thought of sin and the God we worship will be not the God of the prophets and psalmists and of Jesus, but another God. It is not a revised and modernized edition of the Christian God that is produced, but a totally different deity. It would be more honest were the resultant religion not called by the name " Christian," but by some new name.

The Nature of Sin

The confession of sin which is made in the Fifty-first Psalm will serve as a guide in understanding the Biblical conception of sin. We start from the external and gradually go deeper. Sins are transgressions, acts which overstep God's commandments. The law says, " Thou shalt not," and when we break that law, we sin. Then, sin is " iniquity," a word which suggests the degrading and defiling effect of sin upon the soul. Not just an outward act, but always its internal result of staining the inner life, is involved. A man who cheats his fellow man breaks a law of God, but a more serious consequence of his wrongdoing is the indelible mark which his act stamps upon his own soul and character.

We reach a yet deeper level of consideration when sin is defined in terms of personal antagonism to God. " Against thee, thee only, have I sinned, and done this evil in thy sight." The full meaning of sin is not comprehensible apart from its effect upon man's relationship to God and God's relationship to man. Yet how often do we consider our sins in this light? We think of them as individual acts of wrongdoing. Perhaps too we think of our personal defilement. What we do not see is that the really serious aspect of our sins is that we have willfully alienated ourselves from God.

Again human friendship serves as an illustration. If a man sins against his friend, wrongs him in some way, the actual deed is not what matters most. The deed might be such as would pass unnoticed by other persons. The real pain which both he and his friend feel is due, not to the magnitude of the wrong he has done, but to the fact that he has betrayed and broken the friendship. Considered objectively, the deed might seem quite defensible and excusable. Considered from the inner standpoint of friendship, it appears as a betrayal of all that is most sacred.

Accordingly, we must consider our sins, not objectively as individual acts of wrongdoing, but from the inner standpoint of our relationship with God. We have acted unworthy of the fellowship into which he seeks to draw us. Willfully we have driven his presence from us by acts of disloyalty and rebellion. This is our sin: not

just that we have erred and strayed and fallen short
of the mark, but that we have asserted our puny wills
in defiance of God's will.

John Calvin defined sin as pride — not pride as the
word is popularly used, parallel with self-conceit, but
pride as that in man which drives him to insist upon the
execution of his own will regardless of the whole universe. It is like the pride of Satan and his angels in
Milton's *Paradise Lost,* who refuse to bow before the
commands of the Lord God Almighty. There is something of that Satanic element in all of us, something in
our natures which defies God and refuses to accept his
rule. In this we touch the very root of all sin.

All this leads us to the edge of the subject of original
sin, on which certainly much unprofitable nonsense has
been talked both pro and con. For most Christians today, however, it is merely a phrase of bygone days. This
doctrine has been called an insult to human nature, and
an affront to humanity. Perhaps what humanity needs
is to be insulted and affronted and shaken loose from
its self-complacency. At least that seems to have been
the conviction of the prophets and of Jesus. Nor is the
objection valid that it is a pessimistic view. It would indeed be pessimistic were a man to believe in original sin
without also believing in redemption. It is hard to find an
answer to the fact that those who have believed most
firmly in original sin have, on the other hand, cherished

the most extravagant hopes concerning what may, by the grace of God, be made of human nature.

If the essence of sin is the assertion of the individual self in defiance of the will of God, then who can disbelieve that it is by nature the dominant factor in life from the very beginning? The smallest child seeks to impose its will upon its environment and to make all things bow down and serve its little self. As life expands, the self remains naturally at the center. Compromises with other selves are made from time to time, territory being conceded in return for certain advantages and satisfactions. The ruling ego may learn more refined and diplomatic methods of exercising its sway. But it is still self, and not God, that holds dominion over life. Jesus' teaching was that self must be denied before God can get effectual control of a man's life. Self, with all its demonic possibilities, must go out of the center and this place must be given to God alone. Jesus' demand for self-denial contains as its presupposition the doctrine of original sin. So also does his demand for a rebirth. The assumption is that the natural man is not capable of living the life of the Kingdom of God. We are born into a nature which seeks to assert, not God's will, but its own self-centered will.

Jesus' parable of the Unfaithful Steward shows us a little of his view of sin. It is based on the premise that all things belong to God and exist for the purpose of serving his will. Man is not a free lord in life, but a servant under orders. He has a wide freedom as steward to his lord and ample opportunity for the exercise of his own initiative. But he dare not forget that he is a servant and take to himself the prerogatives of a sovereign in life. That is sin — to act as though we were free to do as we liked, to deal with the things of life with no regard for any will beyond our own, to make what has been entrusted to us serve our own ends, rather than the ends of Him who is Lord over us. Jesus seems to take it for granted that we have all been unfaithful stewards in this sense. We have dealt with life in such a way that we owe a debt to God which we can never hope to pay. Here again sin and self-will are the same.

The Inclusion of All Under Sin

The question may be asked whether Jesus merely adopted the conception of sin that he found in the Old Testament or whether he brought to the world a new conception. It is perhaps truest to say that in him the full implications of the Old Testament teaching are brought out into the open. Before Jesus' time, with few exceptions, the idea prevailed that in contrast to sinners there are always the righteous. Religious men of Jesus' own day would agree with him that sin is a terrible thing, calling for repentance and forgiveness, although they would consider themselves by their goodness far removed from any such need. They might occasionally have small sins of which to repent and be forgiven, but never any of such seriousness as to set in question God's favor toward them. They, along with the majority of good people of all generations, had a two-part theory of humanity, separate compartments for the good people and the bad people. Such a theory would be very comforting for good-living religious people like themselves, though very damning and disconcerting for all who failed to come up to their standards. Jesus' attitude in this regard was revolutionary, and yet completely in accord with much that prophets and psalmists had said long before. Refusing to recognize any such distinction, and intensely bitter against those who maintained it, he seemed to regard it as the prime self-delusion of man.

There is a gentle sarcasm in Jesus' words, " I came not to call the righteous, but sinners to repentance." To Jesus there were no righteous persons. We need only remember his words to the man who called him " Good Master." Jesus would not tolerate this easy courteous use of " good." " Why callest thou me good? there is none good but one, that is God." There were some, he knew, who acknowledged no sin and considered themselves righteous. With such he could do nothing. Their consciousness of goodness was an insuperable obstacle to any true work of God through them. Jesus' declara-

tion that his mission is only to sinners does not mean
that any man is beyond the scope of his Gospel. It is a
Gospel for sinners only, and therefore a Gospel for all
men. Jesus' meaning is that every man who knows the
truth about himself knows that he is a sinner before
God. Side by side let us set the words of Jesus spoken
to religious men who were bent upon punishing a sinful
woman: " He that is without sin among you, let him
first cast a stone at her," and the words of John, speaking of himself and others far on in the Christian life:
" If we say that we have no sin, we deceive ourselves,
and the truth is not in us." However far we go in Christian living and however fruitful our lives may be in
Christian graces, we never to our dying day get to the
place where we can cease to beat upon our breasts and
cry out to God, " God, be merciful to me a sinner."

Forgiveness Cannot Be Bought

Belief in the possibility of forgiveness existed in a
crude form in very early times. Primitive sacrifices were
often attempts on the part of man to escape from the
burden of his guilt. He tried by an offering to God to
make right the debt which he felt he owed and so to ob-
tain forgiveness. Modern man, with much the same idea
in mind, gives a special donation to charity or the
Church, or does some kind deed, in order to get a mark

on the right side of God's ledger to balance against the black mark his sin has put on the wrong side. In fact, the average man much prefers to settle his account with God by a sacrifice of this kind rather than to undergo the humiliating experience of repentance. Such sacrifices settle nothing, for they leave the nature of man essentially unchanged. The idea behind them is not to escape from sin, but from the consequences of sin, a purely selfish motive. The belief that God lets a man balance his account in this way gives us an immoral God, a God who can be bought off, and a conscience which no longer is certain of the damnableness of sin.

The prophets of Israel, with good reason, condemned the sacrifices that were offered by the priests on behalf of the people, and insisted that the only sacrifice acceptable to God was a humble and penitent heart. That God is merciful and compassionate they firmly believed, but to them it was an impossibility for God to bestow pardon where no true repentance had come to pass. " Let the wicked forsake his way, and the unrighteous man his thoughts: and let him return unto the Lord, and he will have mercy upon him; and to our God, for he will abundantly pardon." The burden of the prophets' message, from Moses to John the Baptist, is the call to repentance. Sometimes we feel that they were too stern in their proclamations of doom for the sinful nation and that their denunciations of sin show too harsh a spirit, but we must not forget that their single purpose was to bring the people to the place where the mercy of God might be open to them. It was their belief in the possibility of forgiveness, and their knowledge of what was necessary before God could or would forgive, that made them so severe in their demands for repentance.

Forgiveness in the Old Testament and in the New

There are some persons who regard the conception of a loving God as confined to the New Testament. Others narrow down the channel through which forgiveness may come to man, saying that only in the cross is it to be found. Yet if they would read their Bibles with open eyes, they would find that wherever God is truly found by man and touches man's life, there is an outpouring of forgiveness and the heart and life are cleansed. No man can know God without knowing himself a new man by God's grace, with the blindness removed from his eyes and the hardness and rebelliousness taken away from his heart. The God of the Old Testament is a God of mercy, and it is mere quibbling to distinguish between a God of mercy and a God of love. It is high time men stopped talking about the lower conception of God belonging to the Old Testament. There is no perceptible difference between the God and

Father of Jesus Christ and the merciful Shepherd of Israel. An air of superiority toward the Old Testament on the part of Christians is unwarranted, unless they know more about repentance and forgiveness than did the writer of the Fifty-first Psalm — which, we suspect, they do not. It would be a great day for the Church were Christians to understand the conditions of forgiveness and to know the reality of it as that psalmist did.

What, then, is added by the life and teaching and death of Jesus? What necessity was there that a Saviour should come to save his people from their sins, when already men had discovered how pardon and cleansing from sin might be found? What necessity was there that that Saviour should die for the sins of men, that they might be forgiven?

The distinction between the Old Testament and the New Testament in regard to forgiveness may be found in this, that in the Old Testament man seeks and finds the mercy of God, while in the New the mercy of God has become incarnate: In human form God is seeking and finding man. It was not enough that man should believe in the possibility of forgiveness and should know the necessity of repentance in order that it might be his. God's forgiveness had to embody itself in our human flesh, coming to us in a form that could be wounded and broken by man's offenses even as we are. Then from a human heart, also like our own, his forgiveness could reach past the offense to the offender and forgive seventy times seven. No man would ever have conceived the possibility of *that* kind of forgiveness were it not actually there in Jesus Christ. Jesus did not retreat one step from the prophets' stern demand for repentance. Rather he deepened and intensified the demand. But in him there was something the world had never known before. His was a compassion for sinful men which sent him seeking them and which let him be content only when he was finding them and by his pardon creating in them new hearts and new spirits.

The significant thing is not that Jesus said to certain people, " Your sins are forgiven," but that, whether he spoke or not, there was something in his Person that effected forgiveness. In the case of Zacchaeus the only words spoken were, " Zacchaeus, make haste, and come down; for to day I must abide at thy house." Jesus' attitude in speaking was such that it called forth in Zacchaeus a new man, ruled by new motives. Zacchaeus knew as he looked into Jesus' eyes that the lost was found and that a new life had begun for him.

It was God's holiness in Jesus that made men hate their sin in his presence, while in the same moment God's love in him gave them absolute confidence that they could leave their sin behind and begin a new life. We must not separate the two, as though first Jesus' holiness wrought repentance and then to the repentant his love

gave assurance of pardon. Jesus would have had little
use for Luther's rule that to the sinner must first be
preached the law and the wrath of God to bring him to
repentance, and only when he has repented should there
be preached to him love and forgiveness. It was evident
at once to the sinner that Jesus was seeking him in love,
yet never for one moment was it possible for him to
think that Jesus' acceptance of him contained a leniency
toward his sin. In Jesus, hatred of sin and love of the
sinner, rejection of sin and acceptance of the sinner,
were elements of a single mind and spirit, working with
full force upon humanity at one and the same time.

The Death of Christ

We must ask now what special significance the death
of Jesus has for forgiveness. To it the New Testament
attributes a unique importance, claiming that in a peculiar way it secures pardon for us all. Through the centuries it has been the story of the cross, far more than
all Jesus' life and teaching, that has brought men to repentance and to the assurance of pardon.

All through Jesus' life and in all his teaching it was
the holiness and love of God that were seeking to break
through into human life. Jesus' holiness was his obedience to God's will. Thus with every approach of his life
to ours, our unholiness — our assertion of self and repu-

diation of God's will — becomes apparent in the light of his holiness. In the light of what he is we first become aware of the depths of darkness that dwell in us. Until we know him we do not rightly know our sinfulness. Jesus' love is that boundless compassion in him which makes him disregard our sin and take us into fellowship with himself in spite of what we are. In this manner a wholly new basis of life is discovered to us. A new purity and a new righteousness become possible for us in and because of this new fellowship. The change, however, is due, not to the strength of our own wills, but to the holiness and love of Jesus which together work upon us in this new fellowship.

What then, is the special meaning of the cross? Is it not this, that on the cross was enacted the consummation of all holiness and love? In the cross we are confronted with an unbelievable holiness, an obedience to God's will which leaves all mankind standing across on the other side, which sets in sharpest contrast God's will and our will so that we can no longer be in any doubt where we belong. It is perfect love, a love and mercy which would not turn aside even from a cross when the work it sought to make perfect was the deliverance of man from self and the opening of a way once and for all for him to be reconciled with God. Thus, as of old with the prophet Isaiah, it is the vision of God, revelation, which brings man to a knowledge of himself and so to

the place where forgiveness is found. The climax of all
revelation is in the cross. All deceptions are torn aside.
All confusion about where the line is between the human
and the divine is at an end. God is God and man is man.
Every pretension of man goes down before the cross.
The cross, by means of which men tried to relieve themselves of the intolerable pressure which the holiness and
love that dwelt in Jesus exerted upon them, by the irony
of the divine purpose became a lifting up and setting
forth of that holiness and love in such a manner that
they might reach to all mankind.

The Church as the Channel
of the Divine Pardon

We have said that while in older times men sought
and found mercy in God, in Jesus the divine mercy
clothed in human form came seeking and finding men.
Few Christians take seriously what follows from this,
namely, that unless today this same divine mercy dwells
in human form, the purpose of the Incarnation is frus-
trated and the cause for which Jesus lived and died is
lost. The intention of Jesus was certainly that in his
followers should dwell the same power of forgiving
sins that dwelt in him. He stated it explicitly so that
there can be no doubt. There is a false reverence which
causes men to say, " Of course that was one of the mar-

velous powers of the Saviour, but we are merely men, down on a different level from him." They call his power of forgiving one of the attributes of his divinity, and feel it necessary therefore to deny the possibility of it to humanity. The true meaning of the Incarnation, however, is that Jesus was bringing this divine power down to dwell in our humanity.

God has two ways of dealing with evil. The first is to punish it and by making it involve severe consequences to discourage men from it. That, however, merely restrains the evil and leaves the roots of it in man's nature untouched. Therefore a second, more thorough, more penetrating way had to be found if ever evil was to be overcome. That which alone could reach deep enough was forgiveness. Forgiveness, thus, far from being merely a negative matter of letting men off from the consequences of their sins, is a key part of God's strategy in the conquest of evil. It is the only really effective means of getting rid of evil from human life. In the light of this, one begins to understand Jesus' insistence that his followers should have dwelling in them a power of forgiveness like that of God himself. In no other way can a decisive victory over evil be achieved. The love which forgives and the love which seeks the lost are one and the same in God's aggressive plan for the deliverance of man.

In general we Christians have reverted to the Old

Testament order of things in regard to forgiveness. We seek mercy and pardon in God or in Jesus Christ, but the thought does not enter our minds that the divine mercy and pardon, working through human personalities, should today be *seeking* men. In our attitude to sin we also revert to Old Testament moralism. Our primary reaction is condemnation and stern disapproval. We come down hard on sin and sinners that we may uphold and enforce moral standards. Our attitude to " a woman who was a sinner " would be that of Simon the Pharisee and not that of Jesus. In short, we deal with sin and sinners as though Jesus had never lived.

When we take seriously the daring thought which is at the heart of the Gospel, that the holiness and love which are God's nature and which dwelt in their fullness in Jesus Christ can dwell also in us by faith, the Kingdom of God will begin to make more progress in the world of sin. If we were holy with the holiness, not of any righteousness of our own, but of the righteousness which is ours by faith and obedience, we should not need to condemn any man's sin. There would be that in us which would cause him to condemn his own sin. If we had in us the same passion to seek and to save the lost that possessed the soul of Jesus, a love which does not ask men if they deserve it but gives itself to them because they need it, through us there would flow forth the healing, cleansing stream of God's pardon. Every Christian should ask himself how his attitude to sin and sinners tallies with the attitude of Jesus, and what likelihood there is that men in contact with him may come to a consciousness of sin forgiven. The thought is not fanciful. That it seems fanciful is but a sign of how little we grasp the true meaning of there being a Church of Christ. We are the body of Christ, the continuation of the Incarnation and of the purpose of the Incarnation, that God's mercy and love may go out through the world, seeking the lost and carrying to their doors the joyous gift of free forgiveness.

No Forgiveness for the Unforgiving

Over and over again Jesus tried to drive home to the minds of men that there can be no forgiveness for the unforgiving, no mercy for the unmerciful. The forgiveness which many practice is a limited forgiveness. They set a limit to the sphere within which they feel it obligatory upon them to forgive. Simon Peter, when he had forgiven a man seven times, felt that he had done as much as could be expected of him. The generality of men, less virtuous than Simon Peter, would not be inclined to forgive a second time were the offense repeated. Then there are offenses that are considered too severe to be forgiven. How often we hear, " I could forgive him many things, but this time he has gone too far "! The world is full of people holding grudges who nevertheless count themselves believers in forgiveness. Were we to question them, we should find that they expect God to forgive them all their sins, and in a limited manner they count themselves kindly, forgiving Christians. Let them weigh Jesus' words about mercy and forgiveness and they may be startled by the application to themselves. Jesus was firmly convinced that there is no forgiveness of sins for the man who, even in a single instance, withholds forgiveness from his fellow man. He who cherishes a grudge and prays, " Forgive us as we forgive," unwittingly calls down a curse upon his own head.

To hold a grudge, to refuse forgiveness of a wrong, betrays a soul that has not yet seen the depth of its sin and its own great need of pardon from God. He who takes in earnest his debt to God, the sins for which he must one day give answer, the unsatisfactory account he has to render, loses interest in the sins of his fellow men. He is humbled in his own mind to a position where he no longer has the inclination to sit in judgment on other men's sins; if he knows the joy of having his sins forgiven and of being lifted by sheer undeserved mercy into a new life, it will be evident in a new attitude to wrongdoers. Whether the wrong is done to himself or to others, he will have learned in Christ a new way of dealing with it. The attention will not be upon the hurt and the offense suffered, but upon the plight of the offender. The sin will be taken as an unmistakable sign of a soul in need, of another of those lost sheep whom Jesus sought, of another life that has gone crooked and can never get straight again unless in some way there can be brought into it the forgiveness and love of God.

Chapter 10

The Life Everlasting

THERE IS NOTHING peculiarly Christian in the belief that there is a life after death. There seems to have been an unwillingness on the part of man even in the most primitive times to admit that the story of life closes with the event of death. Archaeologists, digging up the graves of men who lived tens of thousands of years ago, have almost always found some objects, such as dishes for food or hunting weapons, which point to a definite, if crude, conception of an afterlife. The later pages of history show more clearly the existence in every part of the earth, among peoples of high and low civilizations, of some idea of survival. The North American Indians had their happy hunting ground. The Greeks had their islands of the blest beyond the far horizon. Sometimes we find a more dismal prospect. To Homer and, closely parallel, to the ancient Hebrews, the life of the dead was a dim, shadowy existence in a bleak underworld, hardly worthy to be called life at all. The point, however, which is indisputable is that man seems to have been consistently unwilling to believe that death is the final episode in life's story.

Natural Immortality
Versus Death and Resurrection

The fact that mankind has always displayed this un-willingness is often used today as an argument in proof of immortality. A vast array of evidence from the history of religions is produced. The universality of the belief is demonstrated; and the matter is taken to be decided by this overwhelming vote of mankind. But thereby essentially nothing is proved. The entire phenomenon may be explained as a protective mechanism developed by man to ease the pain that death causes. When two people who care for each other are parted, it is only natural that the desire to see each other again should be intense. That intense desire is quite capable of producing the conceptions of immortality which we find throughout the world. However, the possibility remains that even this vast majority of men may be wrong. There is no reason for considering the thought of immortality justified merely because the natural desire of man is that it should be so.

It may seem a harsh statement, yet it must be said, that the belief of many Christian people regarding the future life has little about it to distinguish it as Christian. They might almost as well be North American Indians or Mohammedans for all that Christianity has to do with this part of their faith. Their desire is purely and simply to perpetuate in a happier state their own existence and that of their loved ones. From Christianity they seek the assurance that this desire will be satisfied. Their belief in God, their relationship to Jesus Christ, the practical morality of their daily life, stand in no essential connection with their belief in immortality. That belief is held apart as a thing by itself. Just as we assume that on crossing the southern boundary of Canada we shall be in the United States, so it is assumed that when a man crosses the borderline of death he will be in paradise. Religion has no more to do with it than with our crossing into the United States.

Perhaps the protest may be raised that if this belief brings comfort to people in sorrow, if it does anything to ease the pain which death inflicts, it is cruel to disturb it or to suggest that it is less than Christian. After all, whether you believe in a future life as a Christian or as a Mohammedan, it all amounts to the same thing in the long run. But does it? That is the very question we must consider. *How* we believe in a life beyond death is of immense importance, having repercussions upon every aspect of life. In fact, this has been the argument of all the preceding chapters, that beliefs are not mere ideas in the mind but have their bodily content in the whole of life and by their nature determine the nature of life. Thus, for a man to assume the existence of a future life for himself and for others, far from having anything in common with the Christian faith, may be the crowning act of human presumption and egotism by means of which he evades the challenge of the Christian Gospel.

Plainly it must be stated that the Christian belief in the life everlasting is never to be identified with belief in the immortality of the soul. The idea has been widespread in recent years that these two are variant forms of a single faith. When eminent theologians can say that Christian thought is quite justified in using Platonic and other conceptions of the immortality of the soul as the intellectual forms of its faith, it is little wonder that laymen find difficulty in seeing any distinction between the two. Thus there has been an almost complete loss of understanding for the peculiarly Biblical doctrine of death and resurrection, of a life that perishes and a life that is everlasting. In its place there has been substituted the doctrine of the intrinsic immortality of the soul, which had its origin and completest development among the Greeks. Actually, behind these two conceptions lie two completely different religions.

Belief in the intrinsic immortality of the soul belongs to a scheme of things, a philosophy of life, which is based squarely upon man's belief in man. Even though it be insisted that man must fulfill certain moral requirements in order to be immortal, that does not affect the central and essential determining factor — the conviction of man of his own worth as a rational, moral, spiritual being and of his right to be immortal.

In contrast to this, the Christian doctrine of death and resurrection is part of a larger truth in which the endeavor is to remove from man every excuse for believing in himself that he may believe in God alone, which tells him that even as a rational, moral, spiritual being he has naturally no end before him except death. Even in his highest and noblest human achievements he remains corruptible and mortal. The corruptible must *put on* incorruption; the mortal must *put on* immortality; the Kingdom of heaven must *come* right in the midst of the kingdom of the world; eternal life must *become* the life of men now. It is notable that where in the Synoptic Gospels we read of entering into the Kingdom of God, in the Gospel of John the parallel phrase is, " Have eternal [or everlasting] life." Eternal life is the life of the newborn man in the new creation, and it is the gift of God, never the inalienable possession of man. It is no longer possible, then, for man to rest complacently in a comfortable assurance of his own immortality, telling himself that there must be something for him beyond, since he has been such a good man. All the ground is taken from beneath his feet, and he is forced to depend wholly upon the grace of God for his hope of life, not only in time, but in eternity.

The issue, therefore, between the two conceptions,

of the immortality of the soul and of death and resurrection, is not a minor one. The very substance of the Christian Gospel is at stake. Belief in a natural immortality is part and parcel of a religion of works in which man saves himself by his performance of moral and religious duties and needs the grace of God only to assist and to crown his human achievement. The classic forms of such a religion are to be found in Greek idealism and Jewish Pharisaic legalism, between which there is a greater closeness of spirit than we might at first suspect. One thinks of the remark of the acute Greek scholar and earnest Christian Maurice Hutton, that even Socrates was a little too much at ease in Zion.

Every religion of good works results eventually in a complacent moral aristocracy, composed of those who have reason to count themselves most successful in the performance of such works. Allowing for the intellectual atmosphere at Athens and the more pious atmosphere at Jerusalem, there remains nevertheless a certain spirit common to both, and the complacency of the " good man " of our modern day is just one aspect of a religion which, whether men are conscious of it or not, is a blend of Greek idealism and Jewish legalism.

To both Jew and Greek it seemed to be a subversion of all moral standards when Jesus, and after him his followers, refused to regard the fulfillment of recognized religious and moral duties as a sufficient discharge

of one's obligation to God. It was unthinkable that a
" good " man should receive, not God's commendation,
but God's condemnation (and to many today it is
equally unthinkable). The man of virtue, which they
were trying to be, was a goal beyond which their minds
refused to go, and consequently Christianity seemed to
be an overturning of the entire moral order of their
world.

Jesus refused to permit the adjective " good " to be
used of any man, rejecting it sharply even when it was
applied to himself and thereby striking at the accepted
religious order of the world into which he came. To
him the relative moral distinctions so important to most
men had nothing absolute about them at all. The man
of blameless character, with an enviable record of
charitableness and religious zeal, might in spite of these
things be completely wrong with God and lacking in the
one thing which alone could make him alive to God and
to his fellow man. Thus Jesus demanded of men something more than virtue and religiousness. He demanded
that they abandon all their pretensions of religious and
moral superiority, recognize that their relationship to
God was one of hopeless bankruptcy, owing a debt
which all their labors could never discharge, and, taking
in earnest their plight as sinners under condemnation,
cast themselves wholly and unreservedly upon the mercy
of God.

Every religion of works survives by being able to promise men due rewards in terms of moral satisfaction and the assurance of present or future benefits. The promise of a blessed future life enters naturally into the picture and becomes the most powerful sanction of all. But a religion of grace has nothing in common with such an order of things. It includes all under sin that God may be merciful to all. It refuses to recognize human merit as valid in the sight of God, because if man for one moment can believe in his own merit he will withhold that final surrender of his inmost self by which alone his being is laid open to the effectual working of God. Likewise it denies to man the right to believe in his own immortality because this is perhaps the mightiest weapon with which he defends his belief in himself and wards off God's ultimate claim upon him.

Thus what is at stake in this matter is whether we are to have a religion of works, man-centered, or a religion of grace in which man has been completely displaced from the center and God has been acknowledged as the only true center and source of life.

It is in the light of the foregoing, perhaps, that we should understand the long hesitancy and restraint of the Old Testament in respect to a doctrine of the future life. Scanty indeed are the passages which point to a personal immortality, even where faith speaks out most strongly and triumphantly. Are we to believe, as we are

usually told, that in this respect Israel lagged far behind the surrounding nations while far outreaching them
in all other aspects of spiritual insight? Surely it is
more likely that this lag was directly due to the nature
of the faith which it was the destiny of Israel to embody. Had they copied from their neighbors some refined version of belief in immortality, there would have
been introduced with it a belief in God and in man which
would have contradicted and negated the fundamentals
of the unique faith which through them was being
brought into the world. The purpose of that faith was
not primarily to comfort man and remove the offense
of death, but to conquer him and redeem him and, re-
moving the offense of evil, to bring him into his true inheritance of life as a child of God.

Thus, long before there was any hope of a personal
immortality, there was the vision of an eternal order in
which, evil having finally been overcome and all mankind having come to a recognition of God's sovereignty,
perfect blessedness would be realized. But the coming
of that day was never envisaged as the product of man's
moral achievements or as the consummation of his pro-
grams of world reform. That which was to bring it
was nothing more or less than the coming of God in all
fullness into his world as Judge, as Lord, as Redeemer.
Finally, the insight was reached that the soul which
knows God as Judge, as Lord, and as Redeemer, and

by that knowledge is taken into the most intimate communion with him, cannot be separated from him by the incident of death. That belief, so arrived at, was vastly different from the belief in a future life which they might have learned from their neighbors.

Life and Death

The Christian belief might be expressed in this way, that for Christians the dividing line between life and death is placed at a different point from that at which it is placed for other men. We are accustomed to say that a man is alive as long as he can sit up and take nourishment and can make the normal movements of body and of mind. When these functions of the body begin to fail, we say that a man is dying; and when at last the heart has ceased to beat, we say that he is dead. The Christian faith gives an entirely different content to the words " life " and " death." A man may be dead in the midst of life, or, again, he may be alive in the midst of death. Thus, when John the Baptist began to doubt Jesus' Messiahship, Jesus' answer to him was, " Go . . . , tell John . . . that . . . the dead are raised." That was what Jesus was doing day by day, raising the dead to life. The prodigal son in the far country was dead, and his restoration to the father's home was nothing less than a resurrection.

John Macmurray, the English philosopher, expresses this well when he describes all human experience as a struggle between a life-principle and a death-principle. The life-principle is love, in which self has been overcome. The death-principle is fear. Where there is no love, regardless of what else there is, there is fear, a destroying, life-consuming fear. Thus only those in whom love has come to birth are truly alive, and all others, however they may pride themselves upon their excellences and accomplishments, are the dupes and the agents of death.

Death is a far greater and more terrible reality than appears to the eye of man. It signifies, not just the destruction of the body, but the imprisonment of the whole life of man in the darkness and confusion which belong to the realm of evil. Since this is the true nature of death, the fear of it is not to be overcome by reassuring ourselves of the existence of a life beyond the physical act of death, but by an overcoming of the forces of sin and death which hold us in their clutches and by a resurrection through which we become partakers of a life which by its very nature is imperishable. This is what the early Christians meant when they spoke of dying with Christ and rising with him into newness of life. It also explains the tremendous importance for them of the resurrection of Jesus. His resurrection was the triumph of the life that was in him over all the powers of darkness and death which seemed, and still seem, to rule in the outward world. *Not death and fear, but life and love, are the ultimates.*

The Decline of Interest in a Future Life

We must turn now to consider the existing situation in the Church in regard to this aspect of Christian belief. It is a commonplace observation that in recent years there has been a great decline of interest in the subject of a future life. In the pulpits of a century ago, heaven and hell were favorite themes of exposition and Churchgoers were constantly urged to prepare for the hereafter, so much so that many received the impression that that was the chief concern of the Christian religion. A volume of present-day sermons picked at random will exhibit a marked contrast. Only a few sermons have any definite references to the future life. Hell is rarely mentioned, and then usually with apologies. The attention is concentrated almost wholly upon situations of life in this world. This contrast is also noticeable in our hymns. Many written seventy-five or one hundred years ago express their concern with a heaven beyond in terms which present-day Christians find alien to them.

It is common to hear this shift in viewpoint deplored by religious people as indicating a serious decline in religion. It cannot be interpreted in any such simple fashion, however, for the factors that have been at work are complex. With all due allowance for the religious indifference, the gross sensuality, and the materialism of our day, we must look deeper to understand such a decided trend, for it is to be found even among the most thoughtful of Christians.

It was inevitable that there should be a reaction from the earlier overemphasis upon heaven and hell which often became downright morbid. There is a trace of hypocrisy in the attitude of people who look back to the good old days when congregations were sent to their homes in fear and trembling with the very smell of the sulphur and brimstone in their nostrils. " That's what is needed to bring people to time today," they say, with a shake of their heads. They want the sulphur and brimstone for the other people, of course, and not for themselves. They do not consider the children upon whose minds religion, coming in that form, was indelibly imprinted in terms of horror.

I once heard two aged men discussing a minister under whom both had sat in their boyhood days, a man of eminent talents but noted particularly for his hell-fire preaching. The one man spoke with satisfaction of the fact that they two alone remained of all who had ever heard the awe-inspiring sermons of the great man. The answer from the other was blunt: " Sorry I ever heard him." He then described the agonies he endured as a child each Sunday night as he lay sleepless with the ghastly images of that day's depictions of hell returning one by one to his mind. The intention of the preacher was beneficent; the efforts were prompted by the earnest desire to save men from the hell fire. Yet somehow he had failed to notice that neither Jesus nor Paul nor any of the New Testament writers, prompted as they were by that same desire, ever used that means of achieving their purpose.

We need not regret, then, the passing of such conceptions. Yet we must recognize that the pendulum of reaction has swung to an extreme in the opposite direction. So reasonable, so sane-minded, have we become that the idea of a judgment or of a hell no longer has any place in our thoughts. We reassure ourselves of the non-existence of hell by using it chiefly as part of the stage property in the presentation of jokes. The idea grows that everyone has a sufficient spark of good in him so that God will be able eventually in some way to effect his salvation and bring him to paradise. We are even told that any lesser view is incompatible with the love of God.

Jesus will hardly be accused of being ignorant of the implications of the love of God and yet there is no version of his teaching which has come down to us of which judgment and hell are not an integral part. He never encouraged men to speculate about the nature of hell, nor would he have sanctioned the lurid depictions of later ages. His severe restraint in speaking of either heaven or hell as places in a future existence had its reason. His endeavor was to get men to understand that heaven is not merely a future possibility, but a present reality. Likewise hell was not so much " the place to which they would be sent if they were wicked " but the nature of their existence in time and in eternity if they stubbornly refused to let God and his Kingdom come in upon them.

To Jesus it was plain that men every day were choosing death instead of life and were living in the Kingdom of the Prince of Evil instead of in the Kingdom of God. His passion to redeem men cannot be understood except in the light of this consciousness. He knew what it meant that all about him were men who already were prisoners of death and inhabitants of hell. That burden of knowledge pressing upon him gave a tremendous urgency to his mission and to that of his disciples. The lack of that sense of urgency among Christians today arises directly from their forgetting both the present and the ultimate seriousness of the issues of life. They have discarded, not only the idea of hell, but the whole Christian insight into the eternal significance of the decisions of life. No longer do men know that death and hell are the grim and seemingly inescapable realities of everyday existence from which millions are still waiting to be delivered.

There were other factors also in the modern reaction

from older views of a future life. One was the growth
of social thinking and of interest in the improvement of
human society. This was coupled with a perception that
men never really get roused into passion against the
evils which cripple and frustrate their life as long as
they dream of a paradise the other side of death. That
dream is like opium which deadens the pain caused by
such evils and keeps men from reacting forcibly against
them. Thus Karl Marx coined his phrase that " religion
is the opiate of the people," a phrase which stuck in
men's minds because there was so much in their religion
that justified the criticism. Those social thinkers who
still glibly use this phrase to dismiss religion fail, however, to realize that a criticism which was justified in
Marx's day has lost all application to a Christianity in
which otherworldly dreaming has become a rarity and
has been replaced by the passion for social reform. The
concentration of mind now in wide sections of the
Church is, not upon a paradise beyond, but upon a paradise on the nearer side of death. Mention of the New
Jerusalem suggests to a man of the present day, not
some realm of bliss in another world, but a great new
social order which he hopes may soon be brought into
being among men.

Again we are unable to agree with those who deplore
this change and look back with longing eyes to the days
of the " old-fashioned Gospel." The old-fashioned Gos-

pel often encouraged men in a thoroughly selfish type
of religion and embodied an utterly unchristian disregard for social responsibilities. At the same time we
must recognize that the reaction has carried men into
equally unchristian attitudes. When in the name of the
Church the revolution of one section of society against
another is encouraged, and men are told that when the
capitalist order is abolished it will be possible to establish the Kingdom of God on earth, we have come into
a perilous state of confusion.

The truth which is being driven home to the minds
of Christians by the terrible events of our day is that
the command to love thy neighbor, feed the hungry and
clothe the naked, is not merely a demand for private gen-
erosity, but an indication from God of how he expects us
to make the machinery of our world to work. The price
of failure to heed is catastrophe. Yet, even though security from want and fear, from the cradle to the grave,
were ensured for every man on earth, the Kingdom of
God, as proclaimed by Jesus, would still be waiting to
come to them from beyond. There can be no realization
of it by any man except through repentance and rebirth.
To identify the Kingdom of God with any historical
order of society is to deny and to confuse the eternal
nature of the Kingdom and the temporal nature of
every order of society. Replacement of concentration
upon a kingdom which is wholly of another world by

concentration upon a kingdom which is wholly of this world is, even as in the former case, merely a swing of the pendulum of reaction from one unchristian extreme to another.

There is no need for us to be creatures of such a reaction. Rather, if the faith formed in us be not a reflection of some aspect of the spirit of our times but the laying open of our whole lives to all that God seeks to do for us and through us in Jesus Christ, then belief in the life everlasting assumes a new role. It will give us a perspective which reaches far beyond this world and at the same time make us conscious as never before of our immediate duty to our fellow men. We shall know that we have no citizenship in God's eternal Kingdom unless we are willing to take up that citizenship here and now in the midst of an imperfect world and to let all things in our lives come under the rule of God.

The Fate of the Unevangelized

A consideration which has weighed heavily upon men's minds in recent years is the destination in eternity of those countless millions who have lived and died in ignorance of the Gospel. The older view was that, having lived and died without the saving truth of the Gospel, they went down in their multitudes to perdition. A very effective way of enforcing the missionary appeal

was to tell how many thousands each moment were passing into the tortures of hell without ever having a chance
of anything else.

To the average man of today there is something so
decidedly unfair and unjust in that that his mind rebels
savagely. What about the earnest, thoughtful God-fearing man of a non-Christian religion, a man who perhaps
puts many Christians to shame with his virtues? Are we
to say that such men lose the chance of heaven because
they do not happen to have had their life stream di-
rected into Christian channels? For such questions the
answer is best given in the words of Rev. 5:1–3: " And
I saw in the right hand of him that sat on the throne
a book written within and on the backside, sealed with
seven seals. And I saw a strong angel proclaiming with
a loud voice, Who is worthy to open the book, and to
loose the seals thereof? And no man in heaven, nor in
earth, neither under the earth, was able to open the
book, neither to look thereon."

It is not for us to say who can be saved or who shall
go down into perdition. To make a statement either
way concerning those who have died in ignorance of the
Gospel leads inevitably into error. On the one hand, we
find ourselves saying that there can be a Christian salvation without Christ, or, on the other hand, that men
are damned by God without ever being given a chance.
Judgment belongs to God, and we can surely trust his

mercy and his justice and his wisdom more than we would trust our own. The man who asserts that God cannot say to a Buddhist or a Confucianist, or even for that matter to a professing atheist, " Well done, thou good and faithful servant," denies to God the freedom which is His. He can save whom he will, and we know from the mind of Jesus that God's condemnation falls often where we praise, and his mercy and favor may be poured out upon one whom we would condemn.

It is with reason that Jesus sought to dissuade men from pronouncing judgment upon their fellow men. To him that was the assumption by man of a power that does not belong to him, but pertains to God alone. For man to attempt to wield it is like taking into his hands a monstrous sword, with which he injures not only all who are about him but himself as well. We shall fare better if we recognize our proper place, not as judges, but as those who are to be judged. Let us, rather, seek that the way of justification which Christ has opened may be made plain to our own souls and to the souls of all men. Nothing but confusion of mind and faith and life can result from any attempt by us to pronounce final judgment, favorable or unfavorable, upon any of our fellow men.

A Summing Up

All that has been said in this chapter can be summed up in the brief assertion that it is impossible to have a Christian faith in the life everlasting apart from a truly Christian faith in God. Everlasting life is the life of the Kingdom in which God is sovereign, or, to use another New Testament likeness, of the home in which he is Father. He, therefore, who is unwilling to become a subject of that Kingdom or a child in that home can have no share in that life. For those to whom " Lord " and " Father " are not just names for God, but express the reality of what he is to them, everlasting life is more than a future hope; it is their present joy; or, again, it is life as that word receives its content in Jesus Christ. " In him was life; and the life was the light of men."

The life that was in him was imperishable. That life becomes ours in its glory and imperishableness only in so far as we are willing also to let it be ours in its lowliness of spirit, in its self-giving, in its redemptive love. We cannot have the life everlasting apart from Christ. The triumph in us of his purity over our impurity, of his love over our self-centeredness, of his obedience over our disobedience, is the triumph of life over death.

Yet, again, with our minds upon the third person of the Trinity, we have to say that the life everlasting is the life of God in the human soul. When man, with all his religion and virtue and culture, remains closed within his own proud egotism, he remains a creature of mortality. His resistance to God is a rejection of his own truest life. When self is dethroned at the center of life, and God in his Spirit is allowed to take possession of that center and to make the whole life a temple for himself, then our little human lives are taken up into the great divine life and we are made sharers of the glory and the strength and the joy which are the very nature of God. Should God's Spirit go from us and we be left in darkness, it is the darkness of death into which we have fallen. When we humble ourselves before him and he returns, the light which rises upon us is nothing less than the dawn of the everlasting day.

The divine institution of the Church is God's chosen way of carrying forward his assault upon death and hell and of seeking to win men to life eternal. Therefore, the Church fulfills the purpose of its institution, not by its many works, however necessary they may be, but by being a fellowship determined wholly in its life and worship by faith in God the Father, Son, and Holy Spirit. Thus it is a fellowship in which, even as in Jesus Christ, the real line between life and death becomes visible, and the life that is eternal actually confronts men in judgment and in promise. We cannot create that Church, but were we ready for it God could and would create it in us. Then instead of being a religious society, we would begin to be an aggressive mission through whom men would be raised from death to life, and Jesus might again have reason to exclaim with joy, " I beheld Satan as lightning fall from heaven."

The Church tumbles Satan from his throne and delivers men from his deathly toils into a life that is everlasting only as it brings to them the forgiveness of their sins. The Church against which the gates of hell cannot hold out is a Church which has committed to it the power of the keys, to open and to shut, to unloose and to bind. That power it has, not through any formal transmission by apostolic succession from Peter, but through being possessed by the same faith as possessed Peter.

The exercise of the power of the keys must be the chief function of the Church, and not only in its clergy but in all its members. If the holiness and love of Christ dwell in his people through their faith in him, then nothing can prevent it that in the midst of life men will know themselves judged and pardoned. A door will be shut against them, and yet at the same time a door opened into the very secret place of God. They will know themselves bound by their sins as never before, and yet that knowledge will lead to a glorious unloosing. This, and nothing short of this, is the task of the Church, to be the channel through which God himself in judgment and in mercy will come to men and, triumphing over death and hell in their hearts, will make them heirs of his eternal Kingdom.

Conclusion

Conclusion

THERE CAN BE no conclusion to this book unless it has failed as a presentation of the Christian faith. When we can round the whole matter off with a few phrases and feel that we have concluded it at least for the present, this smugness ought in itself to be an indication to us that we have been dealing with something less than the Christian faith. The questions remain open both for the writer and for the reader. If we let them close this side of the grave, it means that we have closed our minds to God. We can never be done with them until we are finished with our earthly life, for life confronts us ever afresh with the dilemma: " Lord, I believe; help thou mine unbelief "!

The book will have succeeded in its purpose if it rouses a few here and there to become watchmen, men who are aware that the faith which is in us determines everything, not only in the Church, but in the world. An unchristian faith must lead inevitably to an unworthy Church, and to a world in which evil will no longer be restrained by the power of faith. When once we know that upon the nature of our faith all else depends, we shall cease as ministers and as people to treat doctrine as a matter of secondary, or even lesser, importance. The place in our study, our preaching, our teaching, and our education of the young, which rightfully belongs to it will not then be so difficult to determine. The day may then come when our Church courts will find time in the midst of their all-engrossing business and their framing of resolutions to ask themselves some searching questions concerning the nature of the faith which has been operative in them. Churchmen will then no longer dare to dismiss as frivolous and vexatious the suggestion that arguments of expediency are insufficient, and that the principle underlying a practical measure of Church policy should be shown to be Christian before it is entered upon. We must become watchmen in the greater as well as in the lesser spheres of life. Though we insist upon the urgency of a right doctrine, it is not as though we ourselves were models of right doctrine. Rather, there has laid hold of us the conviction that there can be no health and no salvation for us unless we are willing constantly to let ourselves be led out of the faiths that are false into the one faith that is true.